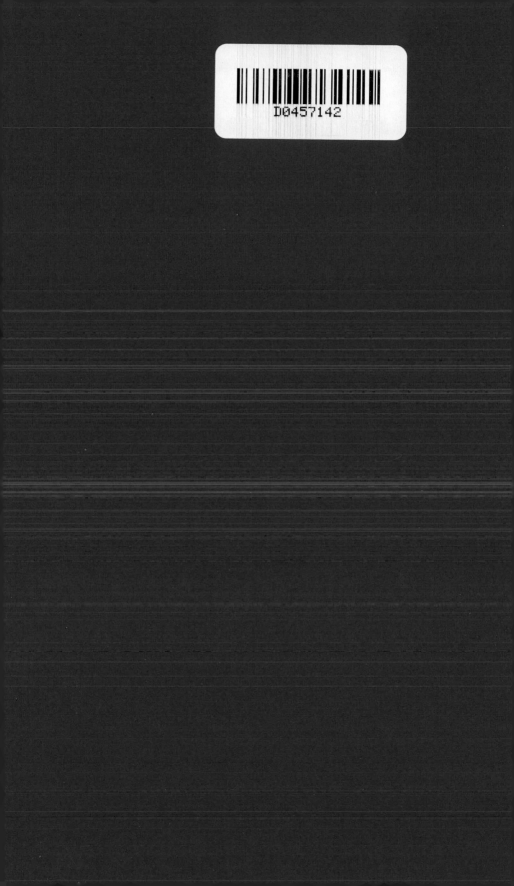

MIND, LANGUAGE

AND SOCIETY

The MasterMinds series:

These concise and accessible books present cutting-edge ideas by leading thinkers in a highly readable format, each title a crystallization of a lifetime's work and thought.

Other books in the MasterMinds series include:

After God: The Future of Religion by DON CUPITT

Finding Flow: The Psychology of Engagement with Everyday Life by MIHALY CSIKSZENTMIHALYI

Machine Beauty: Elegance and the Heart of Technology by DAVID GELERNTER

Future contributors include:

STEWART BRAND
JOHN MADDOX
SHERRY TURKLE

Praise for Basic Books's Science Masters series:

"This is good publishing. PBS, eat your heart out."
—Kirkus Reviews

"Aimed at busy, nonmathematical readers, this precise series evinces solid quality control and begins under highly favorable auspices."
—A. L. A. Booklist

"If this standard is maintained, the Science Masters series looks set to play a major role in the responsible popularization of sciences."
—New Scientist

MIND, LANGUAGE AND SOCIETY

PHILOSOPHY IN THE REAL WORLD

JOHN R. SEARLE

MasterMinds

BASIC
BOOKS

A Member of the
Perseus Books Group

Copyright © 1998 by John R. Searle.

Published by Basic Books,
A Member of the Perseus Books Group

All rights reserved. Printed in the United States of America. No part of this book may be used or reproduced in any manner whatsoever without written permission except in the case of brief quotations embodied in critical articles and reviews. For information address Basic Books, 10 East 53rd Street, New York, NY 10022.

FIRST EDITION

A CIP catalog record for this book is available from the Library of Congress.

ISBN 0-465-04519-7

99 00 01 02 ❖/RRD 10 9 8 7 6 5 4 3 2

For Dagmar

≡CONTENTS

☰ INTRODUCTION

Anyone who writes books on a variety of topics must eventually feel an urge to write a book explaining how the various topics relate to each other. How does it all hang together? This is such a book. In it I try to explain, at least in summary form, some of my views on mind, language, and society, and to explain how they relate to each other, and how they fit into our overall contemporary conception of the universe. Indeed, my first thought for a subtitle was "How It All Hangs Together."

I am partly emboldened to undertake such a project by the generous reception given my 1984 Reith Lectures for the BBC,[1] published in book form as *Minds, Brains, and Science*, which was similarly broad in scope. Both books attempt to address a wide range of problems in a way that is accessible to nonspecialists, but without sacrificing intellectual complexity. The earlier book stayed at the levels of the mind and brain. This one tries, so to speak, to climb up the levels from mind to language and social reality generally.

Both books also exemplify a pervasive contemporary trend in philosophy: for a large number of philosophers, the philosophy of mind is now first philosophy. Problems about language, knowledge, ethics, society, free will, rationality, and a large number of other topics are best approached by way of an understanding of mental phenomena. In my hands at least, they are approached by way of an analysis of mind that rejects both dualism and materialism. I set out to write a book about mind, language, and society, and now that it is finished, I discover that a disproportionately large part of it is about the mind. Given the intellectual basis from which the argument proceeds, that emphasis should not be surprising.

I have borrowed shamelessly from my earlier writings. Friends of those works may justifiably feel a sense of déjà vu at some of the ideas in this book. I can only say that in order to tell you how it all works together, I have to tell you some of the things I have said before.

Several people have helped in the preparation of this book. I especially want to thank my research assistant, Jennifer Hudin; and most of all, my wife Dagmar Searle, who, as usual, was helpful at every stage. I dedicate this book to her.

MIND, LANGUAGE

AND SOCIETY

ONE

Basic Metaphysics: Reality and Truth

The Enlightenment Vision: Reality and Its Intelligibility

From the time of the scientific revolutions of the seventeenth century until the early decades of the twentieth, it was possible for an educated person to believe that he or she could come to know and understand the important things about how the universe works. From the Copernican Revolution, through Newtonian mechanics, the theory of electromagnetism, and Darwin's theory of evolution, the universe made a kind of sense, had a kind of intelligibility, and was becoming ever more accessible through the steadily increasing growth of knowledge and understanding. It was even possible for educated people to feel that scientific knowledge was perfectly consistent with, even an adjunct to, their religious faith. This belief required making a distinction between two metaphysical realms—the mental or spiritual on the one hand, and the physical or material on the other. Religion owned the spiritual realm, science the material. This distinction between the realms of the mind and the body seemed independently justifiable; indeed, it had a long history and received its most famous formulation in the work of René Descartes, a philosopher who was very much part of the seventeenth-century scientific revolution. Even the great "subversive" revolutionaries of the late nineteenth and early twentieth centuries, Sigmund Freud and Karl Marx, though they rejected Cartesian dualism, thought of their work as part of the growth of science as it had been conceived since the seventeenth century. Freud thought he was creating a science of the mind, Marx a science of history and society.

There was, in short, a long period in Western civilization when it was assumed that the universe was completely intelligible and that we were capable of a systematic understanding of its nature. Because these twin assumptions found expression in a series of classic statements in the European Enlightenment, I propose to call them "the Enlightenment vision." The high-water mark of this optimistic vision came in the late nineteenth century, especially in Bismarckian Germany and Victorian England, and two of its most eloquent exemplars were Gottlob Frege, a German mathematician and philosopher, and Bertrand Russell, a British logician and philosopher.

Beginning in the early decades of the twentieth century, a number of events, intellectual and otherwise, happened to challenge and undermine this traditional optimism both about the nature of things and about our ability to comprehend that nature. My guess is that the greatest single psychological blow to the intellectual optimism of the nineteenth century was not an intellectual development at all but rather the catastrophe of the First World War. There were also a number of purely intellectual challenges, however, to the Enlightenment vision. Both the intelligibility of the real world and our capacity to comprehend the world seemed to come under attack from various quarters. First, relativity theory challenged our most fundamental assumptions about space and time, and about matter and energy. How, for example, are we to understand a universe where, according to Albert Einstein, if we went to a star at nearly the speed of light and returned in ten years we would be ten years older but everything on earth would be a hundred years older? Second, the discovery of the set theoretical paradoxes seemed to challenge the rationality of that very citadel of rationality, mathematics. If the foundations of mathematics contain a contradiction, then nothing seems secure. As Frege himself said when confronted with Russell's paradox, "Your discovery of the contradiction has surprised me beyond words and, I should almost like to say, left me thunderstruck, because it has rocked the ground on which I had meant to build arithmetic." It seems "to undermine not only the foundations of my arithmetic but the only possible foundations of arithmetic as such." Third, Freudian psychology was taken not as a gateway to an improved rationality but as a proof of the impossibility of rationality. According to Freud, the rational consciousness is only an island in a sea of the irrational unconscious. Fourth, Kurt Gödel's incompleteness proof seemed to deliver another blow to mathematics. There are true statements in mathematical systems that we can all see to be true but that cannot be proven to be true within those systems. Prior to Gödel, it had seemed that the very meaning of "true" in mathematics implied "mathematically provable." Fifth, and worst of all, on certain interpretations, quantum mechanics seemed simply unassimilable to our traditional conceptions of the determinacy and independent existence of the physical universe. Quantum mechanics seemed to show both that physical reality at the most fundamental level is indeterministic and that the conscious observer, in the very act of observation, is in part creating the very reality he or she is observing. Sixth, in the late twentieth century the rationality of science itself came under attack from authors such as Thomas Kuhn and Paul Feyerabend, who argued that science itself was infected with arbitrariness and irrationality. Kuhn was taken to have shown that a major scientific revolution is not just a new description of the same reality, but that it creates a different "reality." "After a revolution," he says, "scientists work in a different world."[2] And Ludwig Wittgenstein, the most influential philosopher of the twentieth century, is taken by many to have shown that our discourse is a series of mutually untranslatable and incommensurable language games. We are not engaged in one big language game, in which there are universal standards of rationality and everything is intelligible to everybody, but in a series of smaller language games, each with its own inner standards of intelligibility.

I could continue this dreary list. For example, several anthropologists have claimed that there is no universally valid rationality, but that different cultures have different rationalities. Similar versions of relativism have become common in the intellectual movements known collectively as "postmodernism." Postmodernists see themselves as challenging the Enlightenment vision.

Just to put my cards on the table at the beginning: I accept the Enlightenment vision. I think that the universe exists quite independently of our minds and that, within the limits set by our evolutionary endowments, we can come to comprehend its nature. I believe that the real change since the nineteenth century is not that the world has become unintelligible in some exciting and apocalyptic way, but that it is a lot harder to understand for the rather boring and unexciting reason that you have to be smarter and you have to know a lot more. For example, to understand contemporary physics you have to know a lot of mathematics. I will not attempt to answer all of these challenges to the Enlightenment vision. That would require several books. Rather, since my main aim is constructive, I will briefly state why I am not bothered by the arguments I just presented, and then, in more detail, I will respond to various aspects of the "postmodernist" challenge.

First, relativity theory is not a refutation of traditional physics, but its extension. It requires us to think in counter-intuitive ways about space and time, but that is no threat to the intelligibility of the universe. It is worth recalling that Newtonian mechanics also seemed paradoxical in the seventeenth century. Second, the logical paradoxes, both semantic and set theoretical, seem to me to show nothing except certain philosophical errors we can make. Just as Zeno's famous paradoxes about space, time, and motion do not show the unreality of space, time, or motion,[3] so the logical paradoxes do not show any contradictions at the heart of language, logic, and mathematics. Third, Freudian psychology, whatever its ultimate contribution to human culture, is no longer taken seriously as a scientific theory. It continues to exist as a cultural phenomenon, but few serious scientists suppose it gives a scientifically well-substantiated account of human psychological development and pathology. Fourth, Gödel's proof is a kind of support to the traditional rationalist conception that separates ontology (what exists) from epistemology (how we know). Truth is a matter of correspondence to the facts. If a statement is true, there must be some fact in virtue of which it is true. The facts are a matter of what exists, of ontology. Provability and verification are matters of finding out about truth and thus are epistemic notions, but they are not to be confused with the facts we find out about. Gödel shows conclusively that mathematical truth cannot be identified with provability. Fifth, quantum mechanics, on some interpretations, I agree, is a serious challenge to the Enlightenment vision, and I am not technically competent to make a serious assessment of its significance. I want to distinguish, however, between the claim that quantum mechanics shows an indeterminacy in the relation of micro to macro levels on the one hand, and the claim that it shows that reality does not have an existence independent of observers on the other. As far as I can tell, we simply have to accept a certain level of statistical indeterminacy in micro-macro relations as a fact about reality. As far as I can see, however, there is nothing in the actual results in quantum mechanics that forces us to the conclusion that the conscious observer creates in part the reality observed. Such paradoxes are not in the actual *results* of the experiments, but in the varying *interpretations*[4] of the results, and nothing forces us to such a paradoxical and counterintuitive interpretation, though some physicists have accepted that interpretation. Next, efforts to prove relativism about rationality—that all standards of rationality are culturally relative—invariably end up showing the reverse. For example, to establish cultural relativism the anthropologist tells us that the Nuer regard twin siblings as birds and that in certain ceremonies the cucumber is the head of an ox. When he tells how the Nuer make sense of these claims, however, it invariably turns out that he can tell us how they make sense *by our standards* and thus how they can make sense to us.[5] It turns out that the apparent irrationality within a tribal culture can be made intelligible by *universal* standards of rationality.

I will have more to say about Kuhn and postmodernist challenges to the Enlightenment vision later.

In this book, I want to use the contemporary period of confusion as an opportunity to undertake a very traditional philosophical enterprise of giving an account of several apparently diverse phenomena in order to show their underlying unity. I do not believe that we live in two worlds, the mental and the physical—much less in three worlds, the mental, the physical, and the cultural—but in one world, and I want to describe the relations between some of the many parts of that one world. I want to explain the general structure of several of the philosophically most puzzling parts of reality. Specifically, I want to explain certain structural features of mind, language, and society, and then show how they all fit together. My aim, then, is to make a modest contribution to the Enlightenment vision.

Introducing Philosophy

This project may sound unduly ambitious, but in at least one important sense this is an "introductory book" in philosophy: no previous technical philosophical training or knowledge is required on the part of the reader.

Books in philosophy that are introductory in this sense usually take one of two forms, and since this one takes neither, I think it important to make the distinction between it and other such books at the outset. The first and perhaps most common type of introductory book is one that takes the reader through a list of famous philosophical problems, such as free will, the existence of God, the mind-body problem, the problem of good and evil, or the problem of skepticism and knowledge. A good recent example of this sort of book is Thomas Nagel's *What Does It All Mean?*[6] The second sort of introductory book is a short history of the subject. The reader is given a brief account of the major philosophical thinkers and doctrines, beginning with the pre-Socratic Greeks and ending with some prominent recent figure, such as Wittgenstein, or movement, such as existentialism. Probably the most famous book of this type is Bertrand Russell's *History of Western Philosophy.*[7] Russell's book is weak on scholarship, but I think it has done much more to encourage the spread of philosophical thought than more accurate histories because anybody can read it with pleasure and with at least some understanding. I read it as a teenager, and it made a big impression on me. Jimmy Carter is alleged to have kept it on his bedside table when he was president.

The present book is neither a survey of big questions nor a history. Indeed, it is of a type that has gone out of fashion and that many good philosophers would think impossible. It is a synthetic book in that it attempts to synthesize a number of accounts of apparently unrelated or marginally related subjects. Because we live in one world, we ought to be able to explain exactly how the different parts of that world relate to each other and how they all hang together in a coherent whole. I want to emphasize the words *synthesis* and *synthetic* because I was brought up by—and am usually thought of as belonging to—a bunch of philosophers who think of themselves as doing something called "analytic philosophy." Analytic philosophers take philosophical questions apart and analyze them into their component elements. They do what is called "logical analysis." This book contains a lot of logical analysis, but it is also a book in which I put things together. It is a synthesis by an analyst. Building on my earlier writings, I want to explain how certain essential parts of mind, language, and social reality work and how they form a coherent whole.

I have three distinguishable objectives. First, I want to advance a series of theoretical claims, both about the nature of mind, language, and society and about the interrelations among them. Second, in achieving the first objective, I want to exemplify a certain style of philosophical analysis. Philosophical inquiry has important similarities with, but also dissimilarities from, other forms of inquiry, such as scientific inquiry, and I want to make them clear in the course of this discussion. Third, I want to make in passing, so to speak, a series of observations about the nature of philosophical puzzlement and philosophical problems. To put these three points more succinctly: I want to do some philosophy, in doing it I want to illustrate how to do it, and I want to make some observations about the special problems of doing it. At the end of the book I state some general conclusions about the nature of philosophy.

If I succeed in my expository ambitions, almost everything I say should sound pretty much obviously true, so obvious, indeed, that the philosophically innocent reader—the reader the book is aimed at—will sometimes wonder: Why is he bothering to tell us this? The answer is that every claim I make, even the most obvious, will be, and typically has been for centuries, a subject of controversy and even rage. Why is that? Why is it that when we start doing philosophy we are almost inexorably driven to deny things we all know to be true—for example, that there is a real world, that we can have certain sorts of knowledge of that world, that statements are typically true if they correspond to facts in the world and false if they don't? Wittgenstein thought that the urge to philosophical error came primarily from a misunderstanding of the workings of language, and also from our tendency to overgeneralize and to extend the methods of science into areas where they are not appropriate. I think these are indeed some of the sources of philosophical error—but only some of them. I will point out others as we go along, others that are more reprehensible than the sources Wittgenstein gives, sources such as self-deception and will to power.

In any case, it is worth saying what sounds obvious because what seems obvious usually only seems that way after you have said it. Before you say it, it is not obvious what it is you need to say. This book, then, may give the impression that I am taking you along a smooth and open road. That is an illusion. We are on a narrow path through a jungle. My method of exposition is to point out the path and then point to the parts of the jungle we need to avoid. Or to put the same point in a way that seems more pretentious than I intend, I try to state the truth and then state the competing falsehoods that give the statement of the truth much of its philosophical interest.

The Default Positions

On most of the major philosophical issues there is what we might call, using a computer metaphor, the default position. Default positions are the views we hold prereflectively so that any departure from them requires a conscious effort and a convincing argument. Here are the default positions on some major questions:

- There is a real world that exists independently of us, independently of our experiences, our thoughts, our language.
- We have direct perceptual access to that world through our senses, especially touch and vision.
- Words in our language, words like *rabbit* or *tree*, typically have reasonably clear meanings. Because of their meanings, they can be used to refer to and talk about real objects in the world.
- Our statements are typically true or false depending on whether they correspond to how things are, that is, to the facts in the world.
- Causation is a real relation among objects and events in the world, a relation whereby one phenomenon, the cause, causes another, the effect.

In our ordinary everyday lives, these views are so much taken for granted that I think it is misleading to describe them as "views"—or hypotheses or opinions—at all. I do not, for example, hold the *opinion* that the real world exists, in the way I hold the opinion that Shakespeare was a great playwright. These taken-for-granted presuppositions are part of what I call the Background of our thought and language. I capitalize the word to make it clear that I am using it as a quasi-technical term, and I will explain its meaning in more detail later.

Much of the history of philosophy consists in attacks on default positions. The great philosophers are often famous for rejecting what everybody else takes for granted. The characteristic attack begins by pointing out the puzzles and paradoxes of the default position. We apparently can't hold the default position and also believe a whole lot of other things we would like to believe. So the default position must be given up and some revolutionary new view substituted for it. Famous examples are David Hume's refutation of the idea that causation is a real relation between events in the world,

Bishop George Berkeley's refutation of the view that a material world exists independently of our perceptions of it, and the rejection by Descartes, as well as many other philosophers, of the view that we can have direct perceptual knowledge of the world. More recently, Willard Quine is supposed by many to have refuted the view that the words in our language have determinate meanings. And several philosophers think they have refuted the correspondence theory of truth—the view that if a statement is true, it is so typically because there is some fact, situation, or state of affairs in the world that makes it true.

I believe that in general the default positions are true, and that the attacks on them are mistaken. I think that is certainly the case with all the examples I have just presented. It is unlikely that the default positions would have survived the rough and tumble of human history for centuries, and sometimes even millennia, if they were as false as philosophers make them out to be. But not all default positions are true. Perhaps the most famous default position is that each of us consists of two separate entities, a body on the one hand, and a mind or soul on the other, and that these are joined together during our lifetimes but are independent to the extent that our minds or souls can become detached from our bodies and continue to exist as conscious entities even after our bodies are totally annihilated. This view is called "dualism." I think it is false, and I will say why in chapter 2. In general, however, the default positions are more likely to be right than their alternatives, and it is a sad fact about my profession, wonderful though it is, that the most famous and admired philosophers are often the ones with the most preposterous theories.

It is tempting to think that what I have been calling the default positions are what common sense would call "common sense." I think that is a mistake. "Common sense" is not a very clear notion, but as I understand it, common sense is largely a matter of widely held and usually unchallenged beliefs. Though there is no sharp dividing line, what I have been calling the default positions are much more fundamental than common sense. It is, I guess, a matter of common sense that if you want people to be polite to you, you had better be polite to them. This sort of common sense has no opinion about basic metaphysical questions such as the existence of the external world or the reality of causation. Common sense is, for the most part, a matter of common opinion. The Background is prior to such opinions.

Some of the most interesting questions in philosophy are those that arise out of a straight clash or even logical inconsistency between two default positions. For example, it seems to me that people typically talk and think as if they supposed that we have free will of a sort that precludes causal determinism and at the same time that all our acts have deterministic causal explanations. Throughout this book we examine various default positions and give special attention to the clash of such positions. In this chapter I discuss a cluster of default positions centered on the notions of reality and truth.

Reality and Truth: The Default Position

Among the default positions that form our cognitive Background, perhaps the most fundamental is a certain set of presuppositions about reality and truth. Typically when we act, think, or talk, we take for granted a certain way that our actions, thoughts, and talk relate to things outside us. I represent this as a set of statements, but that is misleading if it suggests that when we are actually talking, thinking, or otherwise acting, we are also holding a theory. The set of statements I give you about reality and truth can be treated as a theory or even a set of theories, but when the Background is functioning—when it is, so to speak, doing its job—we do not need a theory. Such presuppositions are prior to theories.

Anyway, when we act or think or talk in the following sorts of ways we take a lot for granted: when we hammer a nail, or order a takeout meal from a restaurant, or conduct a lab experiment, or wonder where to go on vacation, we take the following for granted: there exists a real world that is totally independent of human beings and of what they think or say about it, and statements about objects and states of affairs in that world are true or false depending on whether things in the world really are the way we say they are. So, for example, if in pondering my vacation plans I wonder whether Greece is hotter in the summer than Italy, I simply take it for granted that there exists a real world containing places like Greece and Italy and that they have various temperatures. Furthermore, if I read in a travel book that the average summer temperature in Greece is hotter than in Italy, I know that what the book says will be true if and only if it really is hotter on average in the summer in Greece than in Italy. This is because I take it for granted that such statements are true only if there is something independent of the statement in virtue of which, or because of which, it is true.

These two Background presuppositions have long histories and various famous names. The first, that there is a real world existing independently of us, I like to call "external realism." "Realism," because it asserts the existence of the real world, and "external" to distinguish it from other sorts of realism—for example, realism about mathematical objects (mathematical realism) or realism about ethical facts (ethical realism). The second view, that a statement is true if things in the world are the way the statement says they are, and false otherwise, is called "the correspondence theory of truth." This theory comes in a lot of different versions, but the basic idea is that statements are true if they correspond to, or describe, or fit, how things really are in the world, and false if they do not.

Among the mind-independent phenomena in the world are such things as hydrogen atoms, tectonic plates, viruses, trees, and galaxies. The reality of such phenomena is independent of us. The universe existed long before any human or other conscious agent appeared, and it will be there long after we have all passed from the scene.

Not all of the phenomena in the world are mind-independent. For example, money, property, marriage, wars, football games, and cocktail parties are all dependent for their existence on conscious human agents in a way that mountains, glaciers, and molecules are not.

I regard the basic claim of external realism—that there exists a real world that is totally and absolutely independent of all of our representations, all of our thoughts, feelings, opinions, language, discourse, texts, and so on—as so obvious, and indeed as such an essential condition of rationality, and even of intelligibility, that I am somewhat embarrassed to have to raise the question and to discuss the various challenges to this view. Why would anybody in his right mind wish to attack external realism? Well, that is in fact a rather complicated question, and one that I go into in detail later. Here, however, I want to note that attacks on external realism do not stand in isolation. They tend philosophically to go hand in hand with challenges to other features of our Background presuppositions that also constitute default positions. Along with realism we generally assume that our thoughts, talk, and experiences relate directly to the real world. That is, we assume that when we look at objects such as trees and mountains, we typically perceive them; that when we talk, we typically use words that refer to objects in a world that exists independently of our language; and that when we think, we often think about real things. Furthermore, as I mentioned earlier, what we say about such objects is true or false depending on whether it corresponds to how things are in the world. Thus, external realism underlies other fundamental philosophical views that are frequently denied—the referential theory of thought and language, and the correspondence theory of truth. Thinkers who wish to deny the correspondence theory of truth or the referential theory of thought and language typically find it embarrassing to have to concede external realism. Often they would rather not talk about it at all, or they have some more or less subtle reason for rejecting it. In fact, very few thinkers come right out and say that there is no such thing as a real world existing absolutely, objectively, and totally independently of us. Some do. Some come right out and say that the so-called real world is a "social construct." But such direct denials of external realism are rare. The more typical move of the antirealists is to present an argument that seems to challenge the default position as I have described it, and then to claim that the challenge justifies some other position they wish to defend, some version of views variously called social constructionism, pragmatism, deconstructionism, relativism, postmodernism, and so forth.

The logical structure of the situation faced by the antirealist is this:

1. Suppose external realism is true. Then there exists a real world, independently of us and our interests.
2. If there exists a real world, then there is a way that the world really is. There is an objective way that things are in the world.
3. If there is a way things really are, then we ought to be able to say how they are.
4. If we can say how things are, then what we say is objectively true or false depending on the extent to which we succeed or fail in saying how they are.

Adherents of forms of subjectivism or relativism who would like to reject the fourth proposition are embarrassed by the first, which they feel has to be rejected or, as they sometimes say, "called in question."

Attacks on external realism are nothing new. They go back many centuries. Perhaps the most famous is Bishop Berkeley's claim that what we think of as material objects are really just collections of "ideas," by which he meant states of consciousness. And indeed, this tradition, variously called "idealism" or "phenomenalism," continues right into the twentieth century. This view came to be called "idealism" because it asserts that the only reality is that of "ideas" in this special sense of the word. Probably the most influential idealist of all time was Georg Friedrich Hegel. Idealism's basic tenet is that reality is ultimately not a matter of something existing independently of our perceptions and other representations, but rather that reality is constituted by our perceptions and other sorts of representations. Instead of thinking of our claims to knowledge as being answerable to an independently existing reality, we make reality answerable to our own representations. I believe the most sophisticated version of the idealistic position is found in the philosophy of Immanuel Kant, who thought that what he called the "phenomenal world"—the world of chairs, tables, trees, planets, and so on—consisted entirely in our representations. He also thought there actually is another world behind our phenomenal world, a world of "things in themselves," but that this world is totally inaccessible to us; we cannot even talk about it meaningfully. The empirical world—that is, the world we all experience and live in—is in fact a world of systematic appearance, a world of how things appear to us. So, on Kant's view, as on other forms of idealism, the world of tables, chairs, mountains, and meteors, as well as of space, time, and causation, is in fact a world of mere appearances. The difference between Kant and other idealists such as Berkeley is that the others thought that appearances—or as Berkeley called them, "ideas"—are the only reality, whereas Kant thought that in addition to the world of appearances, there is a reality of things in themselves behind the appearances, of which we can have no knowledge whatever.

Why have so many able philosophers found idealism, in its different versions, appealing? Well, one of its advantages is that it enables us to answer the challenge of skepticism, the view that we can't really know how the world is. Indeed, historically, idealism grew out of failures to answer skepticism of the sort advanced by Descartes. All forms of skepticism rest on the claim that we can have all of the possible evidence for any claim and still be radically mistaken. We can have the most perfect possible evidence for the existence of an external world and still be suffering from a massive hallucination. You could be deceived by an evil demon, or be a brain in a vat, or be dreaming, and so on.* The idealist solves this problem by removing the gulf between evidence and reality in such a way that the evidence coincides with reality. It then becomes a rather simple matter to distinguish those cases such as illusions, rainbows, hallucinations, and so on, that are not real from those that are constitutive of the "real world." Illusions are simply appearances that do not cohere appropriately with our other appearances. But in both illusory and nonillusory perceptions, there is nothing beyond our representations. The appeal of idealism, in short, is that the gulf between reality and appearance, the gulf that makes skepticism possible, is removed. Reality consists in systematic appearances.

I have to confess, however, that I think there is a much deeper reason for the persistent appeal of all forms of antirealism, and this has become obvious in the twentieth century: it satisfies a basic urge to power. It just seems too disgusting, somehow, that we should have to be at the mercy of the "real world." It seems too awful that our representations should have to be answerable to anything but us. This is why people who hold contemporary versions of antirealism and reject the correspondence theory of truth typically sneer at the op-

---

*The "brain in a vat" is a philosopher's fantasy according to which one has all one's experiences even though one consists of only a brain in a vat of nutrients. The experiences are produced artificially by electrically stimulating the brain.

posing view. Richard Rorty, for example, refers sarcastically to "Reality as It Is in Itself."[8]

Fifty years ago it seemed that idealism was dead, and in the version represented by the line that goes from Berkeley through Hegel, this is still largely true. Recently, however, new forms of denial of realism have emerged. As Rorty puts it, "Something which seemed much like idealism began to become intellectually respectable."[9] This comes in several versions, each typically more obscure than the last, and appears under such labels as "deconstruction," "ethnomethodology," "pragmatism," and "social constructionism." I once debated a famous ethnomethodologist who claimed to have shown that astronomers actually create quasars and other astronomical phenomena through their researches and discourses. "Look," I said, "suppose you and I go for a walk in the moonlight, and I say, 'Nice moon tonight,' and you agree. Are we creating the moon?" "Yes," he said.

In the late twentieth century, worries about skepticism have been less influential in motivating antirealism. It is not easy to get a fix on what drives contemporary antirealism, but if we had to pick out a thread that runs through the wide variety of arguments, it would be what is sometimes called "perspectivism." Perspectivism is the idea that our knowledge of reality is never "unmediated," that it is always mediated by a point of view, by a particular set of predilections, or, worse yet, by sinister political motives, such as an allegiance to a political group or ideology. And because we can never have unmediated knowledge of the world, then perhaps there is no real world, or perhaps it is useless to even talk about it, or perhaps it is not even interesting. So antirealism in the late twentieth century is somewhat bashful and evasive. When I say "bashful" and "evasive," I mean to contrast it with the bare, brute, bald assertion that I am making of the default position: there exists a real world that is totally independent of us. A world of mountains, molecules, trees, oceans, galaxies, and so on. Notice some of the contrasting views: Hilary Putnam writes, "If one must use metaphorical language, let the metaphor be this: the mind and the world jointly make up the mind and the world."[10] Jacques Derrida writes, "There exists nothing outside of texts (*Il n'y a pas de hors texte*)."[11] Richard Rorty writes, "I think the very idea of a 'fact of the matter' is one we would be better off without."[12] Nelson Goodman claims that we make worlds by drawing certain sorts of boundaries rather than others.

> Now as we thus make constellations by picking out and putting together certain stars rather than others, so we make stars by drawing certain boundaries rather than others. Nothing dictates whether the sky shall be marked off into constellations or other objects. We have to make what we find, be it the Great Dipper, Sirius, food, fuel, or a stereo system.[13]

What should we say in answer to these challenges to the default position? I will answer several of the most common forms of argument, but I have to confess at the outset that I don't think it is the argument that is actually driving the impulse to deny realism. I think that as a matter of contemporary cultural and intellectual history, the attacks on realism are not driven by arguments, because the arguments are more or less obviously feeble, for reasons I will explain in detail in a moment. Rather, as I suggested earlier, the motivation for denying realism is a kind of will to power, and it manifests itself in a number of ways. In universities, most notably in various humanities disciplines, it is assumed that, if there is no real world, then science is on the same footing as the humanities. They both deal with social constructs, not with independent realities. From this assumption, forms of postmodernism, deconstruction, and so on, are easily developed, having been completely turned loose from the tiresome moorings and constraints of having to confront the real world. If the real world is just an invention—a social construct designed to oppress the marginalized elements of society—then let's get rid of the real world and construct the world we want. That, I think, is the real driving psychological force behind antirealism at the end of the twentieth century.

However, there are two logical points that I need to make immediately. First, pointing out the psychological origins of antirealism is not a refutation of antirealism. It would be a genetic fallacy to suppose that by exposing the illegitimate origins of the arguments against realism, we somehow refute the arguments. That is not enough. Second, since arguments have been presented against realism, we have to answer them in detail. So, here goes.

Four Challenges to Realism

The most common contemporary argument against realism, as I said, is perspectivism. The argument takes different forms, but the thread that runs through them is that we have no access to, we have no way of representing, and no means of coping with the real world except from a certain point of view, from a certain set of presuppositions, under a certain aspect, from a certain stance. If there is no unmediated access to reality, then, so the argument goes, there is really no point in talking about reality, and indeed, there is no reality independent of the stances, aspects, or points of view. A good statement of such perspectivism is to be found in a textbook on the philosophy of social science by Brian Fay. (Often, by the way, we can find out more about what is going on in a culture by looking at undergraduate textbooks than by looking at the work of more prestigious thinkers. The textbooks are less clever at concealment.)

Perspectivism is the dominant epistemological mode of contemporary intellectual life. *Perspectivism* is the view that all knowledge is essentially perspectival in character; that is, knowledge claims and their assessment always take place *within* a framework that provides the conceptual resources in and through which the world is described and explained. According to perspectivism, no one ever views reality directly as it is in itself; rather, they approach it from their own slant with their own assumptions and preconceptions.[14]

So far, this does not seem to be an attack on even the most naive form of realism. It just says that in order to know reality, you have to know it from a point of view. The only mistake in this passage is that somehow or other, knowing reality directly as it is in itself requires that it be known from no point of view. This is an unjustified assumption to make. For example, I directly see the chair in front of me, but of course I see it from a point of view. I know it directly from a perspective. Insofar as it is even intelligible to talk of knowing "reality directly as it is in itself," I know it directly as it is in itself when I know that there is a chair over there because I see it. That is to say, perspectivism, so defined, is not inconsistent with either realism or the doctrine of epistemic objectivity that says we have direct perceptual access to the real world.

The clincher is presented when Fay goes on to say that perspectivism makes it impossible to have knowledge of independently existing facts. Here is how the argument goes:

Note here that it is never phenomena themselves which are facts, but *phenomena under a particular description*. Facts are linguistically meaningful entities which select out from the stream of events what happened or what exists. But this means that in order for there to be facts at all there must be a vocabulary in terms of which they can be described. Without a prior vocabulary which it describes or brings to a situation, there would be no facts whatsoever.

And in the next paragraph:

Put succinctly: Facts are rooted in conceptual schemes.[15]

This whole passage seems to me typical of the arguments used against external realism in contemporary philosophy. They are all bad arguments. It is true that we need a vocabulary to *describe* or *state* the facts. But just as it does not follow from the fact that I see reality always from a point of view and under certain aspects that I never directly perceive reality, so from the fact that I must have a vocabulary in order to state the facts, or a language in order to identify and describe the facts, it simply does not follow that the facts I am describing or identifying have no independent existence. The fact that there is saltwater in the Atlantic Ocean is a fact that existed long before there was anyone to identify that body of water as the Atlantic Ocean, to identify the stuff in it as water, or to identify one of its chemical components as salt. Of course, in order for us to make all these identifications, we must have a language, but so what? The facts exist, utterly independent of language. Fay's argument as presented is a fallacy. It is a use-mention fallacy to suppose that the linguistic and conceptual nature of the *identification* of a fact requires that the *fact identified* be itself linguistic in nature.[16] Facts are conditions that make statements true, but they are not identical with their linguistic descriptions. We invent words to state facts and to name things, but it does not follow that we invent the facts or the things.

A second argument, related to the argument from perspectivism, is the argument from conceptual relativity. Here is how it goes. All of our concepts are made by us as human beings. There is nothing inevitable about the concepts we have for describing reality. But, so the antirealist argues, the relativity of our concepts, if properly understood, shows that external realism is false because we have no access to external reality except through our concepts. Different conceptual structures give different descriptions of reality, and these descriptions are inconsistent with each other. For example, relative to one conceptual scheme, if I am asked, "How many objects are there in this room?" I may count the various items of furniture in this room. But relative to another conceptual scheme, that does not distinguish between the elements of a set of furniture but just treats the furniture set as one entity, there will be a different answer to the question, "How many objects are there in the room?" As an answer within the first conceptual scheme, we can say that there are seven objects in the room. Within the second scheme, there is one object. So how many are there really? The antirealist says that there is no answer to that question. There is no fact of the matter except relative to a conceptual scheme, and therefore there is no real world except relative to a conceptual scheme.

What should we make of this argument? I am embarrassed to say that I think it is remarkably feeble, even though it has been advanced in different versions by some very well known philosophers. There really are seven objects in the room, as counted by one system of counting, and there really is only one object, as counted by another system of counting. But the real world doesn't care about which system of counting we use; each gives us an alternative and true description of the one world, using a different system of counting. The appearance of a problem derives entirely from the apparent inconsistency in saying there is only one object and yet there are seven objects. But once you understand the nature of the claims, there is no inconsistency whatever. They are both consistent, and indeed, both are true. There are many such examples in daily life. I weigh 160 in pounds and 72 in kilograms. So what do I weigh really? The answer is, both 160 and 72 are true depending on which system of measurement we are using. There is really no problem or inconsistency whatever.

A third argument against external realism is the argument from the history of science. This argument has its origin in

Thomas Kuhn's book *The Structure of Scientific Revolutions*, though I doubt that Kuhn himself ever accepted the argument in this form. Science, on Kuhn's account, does not proceed by the steady accumulation of knowledge; rather it proceeds by a series of revolutions: whereby one paradigm for doing science is abandoned because of its inability to solve certain puzzles and as a result of a scientific revolution is replaced by a new paradigm. What you find is not a steady accretion of knowledge about reality as it is in itself, but rather a series of different discourses, each within its own paradigm. Science does not describe an independently existing reality but is forever creating new "realities" as it goes along. As Bruno Latour and Steve Woolgar say, "Our point is that outthereness is the *consequence* of scientific work rather than its *cause*."[17] As I mentioned earlier, I doubt that Kuhn would have accepted this antirealist argument, but he did think there was a sense in which Newton worked in a different world than Aristotle.

What should we make of this argument? I have to say, once again, that it does not seem to me to cast any doubt at all on even the most naive version of the default position that there is a real world existing totally independently of us and that it is the task of the natural sciences to provide us with a theoretical account of how the world works. Suppose that Kuhn is entirely correct that science proceeds by fits and starts and occasional big jolts. Suppose that revolutionary theories are not even translatable into the vocabulary of earlier theories, to the extent that the arguments between adherents of the different theories reveal only mutual incomprehension. What follows? I think nothing interesting follows about external realism. That is, the fact that scientific efforts to account for the real world are less rational and less cumulative than we had previously supposed—if it is a fact—casts no doubt at all on the presupposition that there is a real world that scientists are making genuine attempts to describe.

The fourth argument against external realism, related to the Kuhnian argument, is the argument from the underdetermination of theory by evidence. Consider the move from the idea that the earth is the center of our planetary system to the idea that the sun is the center, from the geocentric to the heliocentric theory. We did not discover that the Ptolemaic geocentric system was false and the heliocentric was true. Rather, we abandoned the first because the second was simpler and enabled us to make better predictions about eclipses, parallax, and the like. We did not discover an absolute truth; rather, we adopted a different way of talking, for essentially practical purposes. This is because the theories were both "underdetermined" by the evidence. We could have held either theory consistently with all of the available evidence, provided we were willing to make suitable adjustments in the theory. The history of such scientific "discoveries" shows that if truth is supposed to name a relation of correspondence to a mind-independent reality, then there is no such thing as truth because there is no such reality and hence no relation of correspondence.

I mention this argument and the example of the Copernican Revolution because I was brought up on it as a beginning philosophy undergraduate in the 1950s. It antedates current debates by nearly half a century. But it is still a bad argument. The shift from geocentric to heliocentric theory does not show that there is no independently existing reality; on the contrary, the whole debate is only *intelligible* to us on the assumption that there *is* such a reality. We understand the debate and its importance only if we assume that it is about real objects—the earth, the sun, the planets—and their actual interrelelationships. Unless we assume there are mind-independent objects such as the earth and the sun, we do not even understand what is at stake, what is at issue in the debate about whether the former goes around the latter or the latter around the former. Indeed, the points about simplicity and better predictions are relevant only because we think of them as ways of getting at the truth about the real world. If you think there is no real world, then you might as well say what you like for aesthetic or other reasons. Why prefer simplicity unless you prefer it for aesthetic reasons? In fact, however, we suppose that the simpler system is more likely to correspond to the facts, because we think that the incredible complexities of Ptolemaic astronomy were really ways of patching up holes and inconsistencies in that theory. The debate and its resolution are precisely arguments in favor of, not against, the existence of the real world, and science as a series of increasingly successful efforts to state the truth about that world. The subsequent development of relativity theory, with its abandonment of the view that sun and planets exist in absolute space, further illustrates this point.

What we choose, when we choose one theory over another on the basis of evidence that is consistent with both theories, is a claim about how the world really is independent of our choice of theories. Quine famously argued that his acceptance of the existence of the particles of atomic physics was a *posit* on a par, as a posit, with the acceptance of the existence of Homer's gods.[18] Quite so, but it does not follow that it is up to us whether electrons or Zeus and Athena exist. What is up to us is whether we accept or reject the theory that *says* that they exist. The theory is true or false depending on whether they exist or not, independently of our acceptance or rejection of the theory.

Any reader familiar with the history of philosophy will be wondering when I am going to answer skepticism, for surely I cannot make these claims about the real world unless I can claim to have knowledge of the real world. The validity of such claims to knowledge would first require an answer to skeptical doubts about the very possibility of knowledge of the real world. So I turn now to what historically is the main argument against the view that there is a mind-independent reality.

Skepticism, Knowledge, and Reality

In the history of philosophy, the most common and most famous argument against the view that there is a reality existing independently of us is that such a claim makes reality unknowable. We are forced, so the argument goes, to the view that there is a world of things in themselves that is forever beyond the reach of our knowledge. But the assumption of such a reality is both pernicious and empty—pernicious because it forces us to the despair of skepticism, empty because you can't do anything with the hypothesis of an independently existing reality. According to Berkeley, if matter does exist we can never know it; if it does not, everything remains the same.[19]

It would take several whole books to do justice to the history of this argument, but here I will be brief. Skeptical arguments in philosophy always have the same form: you could have the best possible evidence about some domain and still be radically mistaken. You could have the best possible evidence about other people's behavior and still be mistaken about their mental states. You could have the best possible evidence about the past and still be mistaken about the future. You could have the best possible evidence about your own perceptual experiences and still be mistaken about the external world. This is so because you could be dreaming, having hallucinations, be a brain in a vat, or be deceived systematically by an evil demon. This type of skepticism (though not all of these examples) is found most famously in Descartes. More radical skeptics go the next step: not only do you *not* have *enough* evidence, but strictly speaking, you have *no evidence at all*, because the evidence you have is in one domain and the claims you are making are about another domain. You have evidence about behavior, but you are making claims about consciousness. You have evidence about the past, but your claims are about the future. You have evidence about your sensations, but your claims are about material objects. Such radical forms of skepticism are to be found in David Hume. The example we will zero in on now is about our evidence for the existence of a real world, or as it is sometimes called, "the external world." How could anyone doubt that he or she is looking at a book, sitting in a chair, seeing the rain falling on the trees outside? The first step made by the skeptical philosopher is to press the question: What is it, strictly speaking, that you perceive when you look at a tree? The answer is that you do not perceive an independently existing material object; rather, you perceive your own perception, your own conscious experience.

The commonsense view that we actually see such things as trees and houses is supposed to be easy to refute. The two most famous refutations are the argument from science and the argument from illusion. Because of the prestige of the natural sciences, the argument from science has been the more appealing in the twentieth century. The argument goes as follows:

If you consider scientifically what happens when you see a tree, here is what you find: Photons are reflected off the surface of the tree, they attack the photoreceptor cells in the retina, and cause a series of neuron firings that go through the five layers of cells in the retina, through the lateral geniculate nucleus, and back to the visual cortex; eventually this series of neuron firings causes a visual experience somewhere deep in the brain. All that we see, literally, directly, is the visual experience in our brains. This is variously called a "sense datum," a "percept," or, more recently, "a symbolic description," but the basic idea is that perceivers don't actually see the real world.[20]

This argument seems to me fallacious. From the fact that I can give a causal account of how it comes about that I see the real world, it doesn't follow that I don't see the real world. It is, indeed, a variant of the genetic fallacy. The fact that I can give a causal account of why I believe that two plus two equals four (I was conditioned by Miss Masters, my first-grade teacher) does not show that two plus two does not equal four. And the fact that I can give a causal account of how it comes about that I see the tree (light photons strike my retina and set up a series of neuron firings that eventually cause a visual experience) does not show that I don't see the tree. There is no inconsistency between asserting, on the one hand, "I directly perceive the tree," and asserting, on the other, "There is a sequence of physical and neurobiological events that eventually produce in me the experience I describe as 'seeing the tree.'"

The second argument is the argument from illusion. This argument takes many different forms, and I won't state all of them, but the common thread that runs through them is this: the person who thinks that we directly perceive objects and states of affairs in the world, the naive perceptual realist, cannot deal with the fact that there is no way of distinguishing the case where I really do see objects and states of affairs in the world, the so-called "veridical" case, from the case where I am having some sort of illusion, hallucination, delusion, and so on. Therefore, perceptual realism is false. The simplest version of this argument that I know of is to be found in Hume. He thought that naive perceptual realism was so easily refutable that he dismissed it in a few sentences. If you are ever tempted to think that you perceive the real world directly, just push one eyeball. If you assume you are seeing the real world, you would have to say that it doubles.[21] That is, if the naive realists were right and I were seeing the real world, then when I see double I should be seeing two worlds. But I am obviously not seeing two worlds. There are not two tables in front of me, even though when I push my eyeball so that the two eyes are no longer focused, I have two visual experiences.

There are many variations on the argument from illusion. Many of them have been, in my view, effectively attacked by J. L. Austin in his classic work *Sense and Sensibilia*.[22] I won't go through all the details now but will just content myself with the general form of the argument and with a statement as to why it is fallacious.

The general form of the argument from illusion is this: If the naive perceptual realist were right, and there really were cases where we directly perceive objects and states of affairs in the world, then there should be a distinction in the character of the experience between cases when we are perceiving objects and states of affairs in the world as they really are, and cases when we are not. But as the two experiences are qualitatively indistinguishable, the analysis of one case should apply to the other, and since in the non-veridical case we are not seeing the real world, or not seeing it as it really is, in the so-called veridical case we must say that we are not seeing the real world, or not seeing it as it really is, either.

Now, once it is laid bare in this form, the basic structure of the argument can be seen to be fallacious. It is simply not true that in order for me to be seeing the object in front of me, there must be some internal feature of the experience itself that is sufficient to distinguish the veridical experience from a hallucination of the object. I take it that the point of the example of the hallucination is that there is nothing in the experience itself, in the actual qualitative character of the experience, that distinguishes the hallucinatory cases from the veridical cases. But why should there be? Since the visual experience is caused by a sequence of neuron firings that begin at the sensory receptors and terminate somewhere in the brain, it is at least conceivable that there should be equivalent neuron firings that produce an equivalent visual experience but without an object actually being there to be seen. If that is right, then the cases where I am actually seeing an object cannot be distinguished from the cases where I am not seeing the object solely on the basis of a single experience in the brain. But why should a single experience be all I have to go on? In the normal case, I take for granted that I am an embodied agent engaged in all sorts of encounters with the world around me. Any single experience only makes the kind of sense to me that it does because it is part of a network of other experiences, and it goes on against a Background of taken-for-granted capacities I have for coping with the world. If that is right, then the single experience, considered in isolation by itself, is not sufficient to make the distinction between veridical perception and hallucination. Again, why should it be? That is, the basic structure of the argument from illusion rests on a false first premise: the assumption that I sometimes see real objects in the real world requires that there be a distinction in the qualitative character of my visual experiences between veridical and non-veridical perceptual experiences. The argument, then, is not sound because the first premise is false.

Once we reject the idea that all we ever perceive are our own perceptions, then we have no epistemic basis for denying external realism.

Is There Any Justification for External Realism?

I have so far been answering challenges to external realism, but can it be justified on its own? I do not believe it makes any sense to ask for a justification of the view that there is a way that things are in the world independently of our representations, because any attempt at justification presupposes what it attempts to justify. Any attempt to find out about the real world at all presupposes that there is a way that things are. That is why it is wrong to represent external realism as the view that there are material objects in space and time, or that mountains and molecules, and so on, exist. Suppose there were no mountains and molecules, and no material objects in space and time. Then those would be facts about how the world is and thus would presuppose external realism. That is, the negation of this or that claim about the real world presupposes that there is a way that things are, independently of our claims.

I have been talking as if these issues about idealism, realism, and so forth, are matters of debate and argument over rival theories. In the history of philosophy, it certainly looks that way, but I believe that this is the wrong way to see the matter. At a much deeper level, here is what I think is in fact going on: external realism is not a theory. It is not an *opinion* I hold that there is a world out there. It is rather the framework that is necessary for it to be even possible to hold opinions or theories about such things as planetary movements. When you debate the merits of a theory, such as the heliocentric theory of the solar system, you have to take it for granted that there is a way that things really are. Otherwise, the debate can't get started. Its very terms are unintelligible. But that assumption, that there is a way that things are, independent of our representations of how they are, is external realism. External realism is not a claim about the existence of this or that object, but rather a presupposition of the way we understand such claims. This is why the "debates" always look inconclusive. You can more or less conclusively settle the issue about Darwinian evolutionary theory, but you can't in that way settle the issue about the existence of the real world, because any such settling presupposes the existence of the real world. This does not mean that realism is an unprovable theory; rather, it means that realism is not a theory at all but the framework within which it is possible to have theories.

I do not believe that the various challenges to realism are motivated by the arguments actually presented; I believe they are motivated by something much deeper and less intellectual. As I suggested earlier, many people find it repugnant that we, with our language, our consciousness, and our creative powers, should be subject to and answerable to a dumb, stupid, inert material world. Why should we be answerable to the world? Why shouldn't we think of the "real world" as something we create, and therefore something that is answerable to us? If all of reality is a "social construction," then it is we who are in power, not the world. The deep motivation for the denial of realism is not this or that argument, but a will to power, a desire for control, and a deep and abiding resentment. This resentment has a long history, and in the late twentieth century it has been augmented by a resentment and hatred of the natural sciences. Science, with its prestige, its apparent progress, its power and money, and its enormous capacity for harm, has become a target of hatred and resentment. This is fueled by the works of thinkers like Kuhn and Feyerabend, who seem to debunk, to demythologize, science. They are taken to have shown that science does not give us objective knowledge of an independent reality, but rather is a series of more or less irrational verbal constructs, "paradigms" within which scientists engage in "puzzle-solving," until the contradictions and inconsistencies within the paradigm lead to its abandonment and scientists rush off to embrace a new paradigm and start over. The picture, in short, of the natural sciences as giving us objective knowledge of an independently existing reality—a picture that is taken for granted in the natural sciences, as anyone with any serious training in the natural sciences can attest—is now much under attack. After saying that science does not give us objective knowledge of reality, the next step is to say that there is no such reality. There are only social constructs.

I need to reemphasize the point I made earlier: my statement that antirealism is motivated by a will to power in general and a hatred of science in particular is intended as a diagnosis, not as a refutation. If it were intended as a refutation, it would commit the genetic fallacy: supposing that explaining the causal origins of a view is sufficient to show that the view is false.

Beyond Atheism

Ultimate reality, to speak rather grandly, is the reality described by chemistry and physics. It is the reality of a world consisting of entities we find it convenient—if not entirely accurate—to call "particles" that exist in fields of force. That view itself is not realism, but it is a claim about how, within the realist Background, the world turned out. Realism is a Background presupposition that says: there is a way that things are. Physics is a discipline that contains theories. The theories say: this is how things are. Antirealists, in challenging the Background presupposition, challenge not so much the theory but the status of the theory. Because there is no way-that-things-are, independently of us, physics cannot be telling us how they are. Physics is just one social construct among others.

But, somebody will surely say, what about God? If God exists, then surely He is the ultimate reality, and physics and all the rest are dependent on God, dependent not only for their initial creation but for their continued existence.

In earlier generations, books like this one would have had to contain either an atheistic attack on or a theistic defense of traditional religion. Or at the very least, the author would have had to declare a judicious agnosticism. Two authors who wrote in a spirit in some ways similar to mine, John Stuart Mill and Bertrand Russell, mounted polemical and eloquent attacks on traditional religion. Nowadays nobody bothers, and it is considered in slightly bad taste to even raise the question of God's existence. Matters of religion are like matters of sexual preference: they are not to be discussed in public, and even the abstract questions are discussed only by bores.

What has happened? I think that most people would suppose there has been a decline of religious faith among the more educated sections of the population in Western Europe and North America. Perhaps that is true, but it seems to me that the religious *urge* is as strong as ever and takes all sorts of strange forms. I believe that something much more radical than a decline in religious faith has taken place. For us, the educated members of society, the world has become demystified. Or rather, to put the point more precisely, we no longer take the mysteries we see in the world as expressions of supernatural meaning. We no longer think of odd occurrences as cases of God performing speech acts in the language of miracles. Odd occurrences are just occurrences we do not understand. The result of this demystification is that we have gone beyond atheism to a point where the issue no longer matters in the way it did to earlier generations. For us, if it should turn out that God exists, that would have to be a fact of nature like any other. To the four basic forces in the universe—gravity, electromagnetism, weak and strong nuclear forces—we would add a fifth, the divine force. Or more likely, we would see the other forces as forms of the divine force. But it would still be all physics, albeit divine physics. If the supernatural existed, it too would have to be natural.

A couple of examples illustrate the change in our point of view. When I taught as a visiting professor at the University of Venice, I used to walk to a charming Gothic church, the Church of the Madonna del Orto. The original plan had been to call the church San Christoforo, but during its construction, a statue of the Madonna was found in the adjoining orchard, and it was assumed to have fallen out of heaven. A statue of the Madonna fallen out of heaven into the orchard of the very church grounds was miracle enough to warrant the name change to the Church of the Madonna of the Orchard. Here is the point of the story: if today a statue were found near a building site, no one would say it had fallen out of heaven. Even if the statue were found in the gardens of the Vatican, the church authorities would not claim it had fallen out of heaven. That is not a possible thought for us because, in a sense, we know too much.

Another example, also from Italy. When I taught at the University of Florence, my parish church, if I may so describe it, was San Miniato, located on a hill overlooking the city, and one of the most stunning edifices in all of Florence. Why so named? Well, it seems that San Miniato was one of the first Christian martyrs in the history of the city. He was executed by the Roman authorities in the third century, about 250 A.D., under the Emperor Decius. He survived the assault of the lions in the arena, but his head was then cut off. After his decapitation, he got up, tucked his head under his arm, and marched out of the arena, across the river, and out of town. He climbed up the hill on the south side of the Arno, still carrying his head, until he reached the top, where he sat down. On that site the church now stands. Today's guidebooks are rather bashful about telling this story, and most do not recount it at all. The point is not that we believe it is false, but that we don't even take it seriously as a possibility.

Another recent bit of evidence of the demystification of the world was the test of the Shroud of Turin. The miraculous shroud, bearing the image of Christ taken from his crucified body, was subjected by the church authorities to radioactive tests and found to be a mere seven hundred years old. Subsequent evidence indicated an earlier date, and the exact date may still be in doubt. But, and this is the point, why do we assume the tests are more to be believed than the miracle? Why should God's miracle be answerable to carbon 14?

The fact that the world has become demystified to the point that religion no longer matters in the public way that it once did shows not so much that we are all becoming atheists but that we have moved beyond atheism to a point where the issues have a different meaning for us.

The impatient reader may well wonder when I am going to take a stand on the existence of God. Actually, I think the best remark on this question was made by Bertrand Russell at a dinner I attended as an undergraduate. Since this incident has passed into legend, and since a similar incident occurred on another occasion when I was not present, I think I should tell the reader what actually happened as I remember it.

Periodically, every two years or so, the Voltaire Society, a society of intellectually inclined undergraduates at Oxford, held a banquet with Bertrand Russell—the official patron of the society. On the occasion in question, we all went up to London and had dinner with Russell at a restaurant. He was then in his mideighties, and had a reputation as a famous atheist. To many of us, the question seemed pressing as to what sort of prospects for immortality Russell entertained, and we put it to him: Suppose you have been wrong about the existence of God. Suppose that the whole story were true, and that you arrived at the Pearly Gates to be admitted by Saint Peter. Having denied God's existence all your life, what would you say to . . . Him? Russell answered without a moment's hesitation. "Well, I would go up to Him, and I would say, 'You didn't give us enough evidence!'"

TWO

How We Fit into the Universe: The Mind as a Biological Phenomenon

Three Features of Consciousness

In the last chapter, we were primarily concerned with the idea that *there is a way that things are* in the world that is independent of our representations of how they are. This view, which I have called "external realism," is not to be thought of as a theory or an opinion. It is rather a Background presupposition, something that is taken for granted by us when we perform many sorts of intentional actions—as, for example, when we eat, walk, or drive a car. It is also taken for granted by us in large stretches of our discourse, indeed, in all of those forms of discourse that are, or at least purport to be, about objects and states of affairs in the world independent of us, all those forms of explaining, stating, describing, ordering, requesting, promising, and so on, that are about features of the real world.

Only near the end of the first chapter did we begin to discuss *how things really are* in the world. At this point, we are no longer dealing with matters of philosophical analysis but actually discussing some of the results of modern science. As far as we know anything at all about how the world works, there are two propositions of modern science that are not, so to speak, up for grabs. They are not optional. It might turn out in the end that they are false, but given the overwhelming amount of evidence for them, they are not seriously in dispute among educated members of our civilization at the turn of the millennium. These are the atomic theory of matter and the evolutionary theory of biology. On the basis of these theories, we can say the following: the universe consists entirely of entities that we find it convenient, if not strictly accurate, to call "particles" in fields of force. These particles are often organized into systems. The boundaries of a system are set by its causal relations. Examples of systems are mountains, glaciers, trees, planets, galaxies, animals, and molecules. Some of those systems are carbon-based organic systems, and among these organic systems are organisms that exist today as members of species that have evolved over long periods of time. The point at which our discussion in this book enters into the story of physics, chemistry, and biology is the point at which some of those types of organic systems have evolved nervous systems, and those nervous systems have evolved what we call "minds," human and animal minds. The notion of a mind is somewhat confused and lamentable, but as T. S. Eliot said, "I gotta use words when I talk to you." This is a word for which we do not really have an alternative in English, though I am going to suggest some other terms that will, I hope, prove more useful than the notion of "mind."

The primary and most essential feature of minds is consciousness. By "consciousness" I mean those states of sentience or awareness that typically begin when we wake up in the morning from a dreamless sleep and continue throughout the day until we fall asleep again. Other ways in which consciousness can cease is if we die, go into a coma, or otherwise become "unconscious." Consciousness comes in a very large number of forms and varieties. The essential features of consciousness, in all its forms, are its inner, qualitative, and subjective nature in the special senses of these words that I explain in a moment.

But first, let's remind ourselves of the enormous variety of our conscious experiences. Think, for example, of the differences between these experiences—the smell of a rose, the taste of wine, a pain in the lower back, a sudden memory of a fall day ten years ago, reading a book, thinking about a philosophical problem, worrying about income taxes, waking up in the middle of the night filled with aimless anxiety, feeling a sudden rage at the bad driving of other drivers on the freeway, being overwhelmed by sexual lust, having pangs of hunger at the sight of exquisitely prepared food, wishing to be somewhere else, and feeling bored while waiting in a line. All of these are forms of consciousness, and though they were chosen precisely to illustrate variety, they do not begin to exhaust the actual varieties of conscious experiences. Indeed, during all of our waking lives, as well as when dreaming during sleep, we are in one or more forms of consciousness, and the conscious states have all the variety of those waking lives.

Even with all this color and variety, however, there are three features common to all conscious states: they are inner, qualitative, and subjective in special senses of these words. Let us consider these features in order. Conscious states and processes are *inner* in a very ordinary spatial sense in that they go on inside my body, and specifically inside my brain. Consciousness can no more lie around separate from my brain than the liquidity of water can be separated from the water, or the solidity of the table from the table. Consciousness necessarily occurs inside an organism or some other system. Consciousness is also inner in a second sense, and that is that any one of our conscious states exists only as an element in a sequence of such states. One has conscious states such as pains and thoughts only as a part of living a conscious life, and each state has the identity it has only in relation to other such states. My thought, for example, about a ski race I ran long ago, is only that very thought because of its position in a complex network of other thoughts, experiences, and memories. My mental states are internally related to each other in the sense that in order for a mental state to be that state with that character it has to stand in certain relation to other states, just as the whole system of states has to be related to the real world. For example, if I really remember running the ski race, then there must actually have been a running of the ski race by me, and that running of the ski race by me must cause my present memory of it. Thus, the ontology—the very existence of my conscious states—involves their being part of a sequence of complex conscious states that constitutes my conscious life.

Conscious states are *qualitative* in the sense that for each conscious state there is a certain way that it feels, there is a certain qualitative character to it. Thomas Nagel made this point years ago by saying that for every conscious state there is something that it is like to be in that conscious state.[1] There is something that it is like to drink red wine, and it is quite different from what it is like to listen to music. In that sense, there is nothing it is like to be a house or a tree, because such entities are not conscious.

Finally, and most importantly for our discussion, conscious states are *subjective* in the sense that they are always experienced by a human or animal subject. Conscious states, therefore, have what we might call a "first-person ontology." That is, they exist only from the point of view of some agent or organism or animal or self that has them. Conscious states have a first-person mode of existence. Only as experienced by some agent—that is, by a "subject"—does a pain exist.

Objective entities such as mountains have a third-person mode of existence. Their existence does not depend on being experienced by a subject.

One consequence of the subjectivity of conscious states is that my states of consciousness are accessible to me in a way that they are not accessible to you. I have access to my pains in a way that you do not have access to my pains, but you have access to your pains in a way that I do not have access to those pains. By access, in the preceding sentence, I do not mean simply epistemic access. It is not just that I can know my own pains better than I can know your pains. On the contrary, for some feelings, such as envy or jealousy, other people are frequently in a better position to know that the agent has the feeling than the agent who is experiencing the feeling. For many such states, we sometimes know about other people's feelings better than we know about our own. The sense in which I have an access to my states that is different from that of others is not primarily epistemic. It is not just how I know about them, though subjectivity has epistemic consequences; rather, each of my conscious states exists only as the state it is because it is experienced by me, the subject. And it is thus part of the sequence of states that constitutes my conscious life, as we saw in our discussion of the inner character of conscious states.

It is often argued that subjectivity prevents us from having a scientific account of consciousness, that subjectivity puts consciousness beyond the reach of scientific investigation. But typically, the argument rests on a bad syllogism. By exposing the fallacy in this syllogism, I believe we can come to understand subjectivity better. Here is how the argument goes:

1. Science is by definition objective (as opposed to subjective).
2. Consciousness is by definition subjective (as opposed to objective).
3. Therefore, there can be no science of consciousness.

This argument commits a fallacy, namely, the fallacy of ambiguity over the words *subjective* and *objective*. These words have different senses, which are confused in this syllogism. In what is, perhaps, the most commonsense notion of "subjectivity," and of the distinction between "subjective" and "objective," a statement is considered objective if it can be known to be true or false independently of the feelings, attitudes, and prejudices of people. A statement is epistemically subjective if its truth depends essentially on the attitudes and feelings of observers. I call this sense of the words—and of this distinction between objectivity and subjectivity—"epistemic objectivity" and "epistemic subjectivity." Thus, the statement "Rembrandt was born in 1609" is epistemically objective because we can know as a matter of fact whether it is true or false regardless of how we feel about it. The statement "Rembrandt was a better painter than Rubens" is not in that way epistemically objective because its truth is, as they say, a matter of taste or opinion. Its truth or falsity depends on the attitudes, preferences, and evaluations of observers. This is the epistemic sense of the objective-subjective distinction.

But there is a different sense of these words and the correlated distinction that I call the ontological sense. Whereas the epistemic sense applies to statements, the ontological sense refers to the status of the mode of existence of types of entities in the world. Mountains and glaciers have an *objective mode of existence* because their mode of existence does not depend on being experienced by a subject. But pains, tickles, and itches, as well as thoughts and feelings, have a *subjective mode of existence* because they exist only as experienced by some human or animal subject. The fallacy in the argument was to suppose that because states of consciousness have an ontologically subjective mode of existence, they cannot be studied by a science that is epistemically objective. But that conclusion doesn't follow. The pain in my toe is ontologically subjective, but the statement "JRS now has a pain in his toe" is not epistemically subjective. It is a simple matter of (epistemically) objective fact, not a matter of (epistemically) subjective opinion. So the fact that consciousness has a subjective mode of existence does not prevent us from having an objective science of consciousness. Science is indeed epistemically objective in the sense that scientists try to discover truths that are independent of anyone's feelings, attitudes, or prejudices. Such epistemic objectivity does not, however, preclude ontological subjectivity as a domain of investigation.

A Clash of Default Positions: The Mind-Body Problem

Consciousness has for many centuries seemed to philosophers to pose a serious problem in metaphysics. How is it possible that a world consisting entirely of material particles in fields of force can contain systems that are conscious? If you think of consciousness as some separate, mysterious kind of phenomenon, distinct from material or physical reality, then it looks like you are forced to what is traditionally called "dualism," the idea that there are two basically different kinds of phenomena or entities in the universe. But if you try to deny dualism and deny that consciousness exists as something irreducibly subjective, then it looks like you are forced to materialism. You are forced to think that consciousness, as I have described it, and as we all in fact experience it, does not really exist. If you are a materialist, then you are forced to say that there really isn't such a thing as consciousness with a first-person, subjective ontology. Many materialists continue to use the vocabulary of consciousness, but it is quite clear that they mean something different by it. Both of these views, dualism and materialism, are quite common in philosophy to this very day.

Dualism comes in two flavors, *substance* dualism and *property* dualism. According to substance dualism, there are two radically different kinds of entities in the universe, material objects and immaterial minds. This view goes back to ancient times, but it was most famously advocated by René Descartes in the seventeenth century; indeed, substance dualism is sometimes called Cartesian dualism, after him. Property dualism is the view that there are two kinds of properties of objects that are metaphysically distinct. There are physical properties, such as weighing three pounds, and mental properties, such as being in pain. All forms of dualism share the view that the two types are mutually exclusive. If it is mental, it can't, *qua* mental, be physical; if it is physical, it can't, *qua* physical, be mental.

Many philosophers today still adhere to some form of dualism, though it is usually property dualism rather than substance dualism. But most practicing philosophers, I think, adhere to some form of materialism. They do not believe there is such a thing as consciousness "over and above" the physical features of the physical world. Materialism comes in many different varieties, and I won't even try to list all of them, but here are some of the most famous examples:

Behaviorism says that mind reduces to behavior and dispositions to behavior. For example, to be in pain is just to engage in pain behavior or to be disposed to engage in such behavior.

Physicalism says that mental states are just brain states. For example, to be in pain is just to have your C-fibers stimulated.

Functionalism says mental states are defined by their causal relations. According to functionalism, any state of a physical system, whether a brain or anything else, that stands in the right causal relations to input stimuli, to other functional states of the system, and to output behavior, is a mental state. For example, to be in pain is to be in a state that is caused by certain sorts of stimulation of the peripheral nerve endings and, in turn, causes certain sorts of behavior and certain sorts of other functional states.

Strong Artificial Intelligence says minds are just computer programs implemented in brains, and perhaps in other sorts of computers as well. For example, to be in pain is just to be implementing the computer program for pain.

In spite of this variety, all contemporary forms of materialism known to me share the objective of trying to get rid of mental phenomena in general and consciousness in particular, as normally understood, by reducing them to some form of the physical or material. Each of the forms of materialism I have mentioned is a "nothing but" theory: each denies, for example, that pains are inner, qualitative, subjective mental phenomena and claims, to the contrary, that they are "nothing but"—behavior, computational states, and so on.

Neither dualism, whether substance or property dualism, nor materialism in any of its many forms seems to me to have a chance of being right, and the fact that we continue to pose and try to answer these questions in the antique and obsolete vocabulary of "mental" and "physical," "mind" and "body," should be a tip-off that we are making some fundamental conceptual mistake in how we are formulating the questions and the answers. On the one hand, dualism in any form makes the status and existence of consciousness utterly mysterious. How, for example, are we to think of any sort of causal interaction between consciousness and the physical world? Having postulated a separate mental realm, the dualist cannot explain how it relates to the material world we all live in. On the other hand, materialism seems obviously false: it ends up denying the existence of consciousness and thus denying the existence of the phenomenon that gives rise to the question in the first place. Is there a way out? Is there an alternative between the Scylla of dualism and the Charybdis of materialism? I think there is.

I hope it is clear that this debate is a clash of default positions. I have presented each in an unflattering light, but look how attractive they can be made to seem. On the one hand, it seems obvious that we have both a mind and a body, or at least that in our lives there are both physical and mental features. On the other hand, we just seem to know that the world consists entirely of physical particles and their physical properties, including the physical properties of large organizations of particles.

We will not fully understand the persistence of the mind-body problem or the appeal of the rival positions unless we see the force behind each of the clashing default positions. Dualism seems consistent with common sense. As Descartes himself said, we all have our own conscious experiences, and we can easily see that these are different from the material world that surrounds us. We each have our inner thoughts, feelings, pains, tickles, itches, and visual perceptions. In addition, there is a world of objectively existing, three-dimensional material objects, a world of chairs, tables, trees, mountains, and waterfalls. What could be more different?

Furthermore, when we think about the relation of our conscious selves to our bodies, it just seems too horrible to think that there is nothing to our selves except our bodies. It seems too awful to think that when my body is destroyed, I will cease to exist; and even if in moments of great courage I can accept my own future nonexistence, it is much harder to accept the ultimate extinction of the people I most deeply love and admire. It seems too horrible to contemplate that such wonderful people will simply be annihilated with the inevitable death, decay, and destruction of their bodies, which, after all, are just material objects in the world like any others. Dualism, in short, not only is consistent with the most obvious interpretation of our experiences but it also satisfies a very deep urge we have for survival.

I used to think that dualism might be a special product of Western culture, but when I lectured in a symposium in

Bombay, on the same platform as the Dalai Lama, I discovered to my surprise that he believed in a version of dualism. "Each of us is both a mind and a body," he began his speech.

Materialism, on the other hand, is also overwhelmingly convincing. We now have several centuries of scientific advance, and if there is one thing we know it is that the world consists entirely of physical particles in fields of force. If we suppose that there are such things as real conscious phenomena, how are we supposed to think they fit into the world of material particles? Are we to think that souls run in and out among the molecules, or are we to think that somehow the soul is attached to the brain, stuck onto it by some metaphysical glue, and that when we die the soul becomes detached? It seems that the only way we can account for our own existence, consistent with what we know about the world from science, is to recognize that everything is material. There isn't anything in addition to material reality—there is nothing "over and above" material reality.

This is typical of philosophical problems that seem insoluble. We are presented with two inconsistent alternatives neither of which it seems possible to abandon. But, we are told, we must choose one. The history of the subject then becomes a battle between the two sides. In the case of consciousness and the mind-body problem, we were told that we had to choose between dualism, which insists on the irreducibility of the mental, and materialism, which insists that consciousness must be reducible, and hence eliminable, in favor of some purely physical existence of the mind. As traditionally understood, both default positions have implications that seem, frankly, preposterous. That is—and this again is typical of apparently insoluble philosophical problems—we start with a position that seems commonsensical, but when we work out its implications, the position appears to have unacceptable consequences. Thus, the implication of the commonly accepted default view that each of us is both a mind and a body, when worked out in the traditional way, is that our consciousness is floating free from the physical world and is not a part of our ordinary biological lives. The default position of materialism is that the world is made up entirely of material or physical entities. The implication, when you work it out the way materialists usually do, is that consciousness, as something irreducibly mental, does not exist. Materialists, after a lot of beating around the bush, do typically end up by denying the existence of consciousness, even though most of them are too embarrassed to come right out and say: "Consciousness does not exist. No human or animal has ever been conscious." Instead, they redefine "consciousness" so that it no longer refers to inner, qualitative, subjective mental states but rather to some third-person phenomena, phenomena that are neither inner, qualitative, nor subjective in the senses I have explained. Consciousness is reduced to the behavior of the body, to computational states of the brain, information processing, or functional states of a physical system. Daniel Dennett is typical of materialists in this regard. Does consciousness exist for Dennett? He would never deny it. And what is it? Well, it is a certain bunch of computer programs implemented in the brain.[2]

Such answers, I am afraid, will not do. Consciousness is an inner, subjective, first-person, qualitative phenomenon. Any account of consciousness that leaves out these features is not an account of consciousness but of something else.

I believe the correct way to solve this problem is to reject both alternatives. Both dualism and materialism rest on a series of false assumptions. The main false assumption is that if consciousness is really a subjective, qualitative phenomenon, then it cannot be part of the material, physical world. And indeed, given the way the terms have been defined since the seventeenth century, that assumption is true by definition. The way Descartes defined "mind" and "matter," they are mutually exclusive. If something is mental, it cannot be physical; if it is physical, it cannot be mental. I am suggesting that we must abandon not only these definitions but also the traditional categories of "mind," "consciousness," "matter," "mental," "physical," and all the rest as they are traditionally construed in our philosophical debates.

Look what happens when we try to stick to the traditional definitions. Consciousness is a biological process that occurs in the brain in the way that digestion is a biological process that occurs in the stomach and the rest of the digestive tract. So it looks like consciousness is material and we have a materialist account. But wait! Consciousness has a first-person ontology and so cannot be material, because material things and processes all have a third-person objective ontology. So it looks like consciousness is mental and we have a dualist account.

If we accept these definitions, we have a contradiction. The solution is to abandon the definitions. We now know enough biology to know that these definitions are inadequate to the facts. *It is always a good idea to remind ourselves of the facts, to remind ourselves of what we actually know.* We know for a fact that all of our conscious states are caused by brain processes. This proposition is not up for grabs. There is a mystery that many philosophers are impressed by—how brain processes *could* cause consciousness—and there is, I think, a more serious mystery, faced by neurobiologists—how brain processes *do in fact* cause consciousness. But one thing we have to accept before we ever get going in this discussion is that, in fact, brain processes do cause consciousness. That leaves us with the next question: What is this consciousness that they cause, and doesn't the causal relation between consciousness and brain processes force us into dualism—a dualism of the material brain processes that act as cause and the nonmaterial subjective processes of consciousness that are the effects?

I do not think we are forced to either dualism or materialism. The point to remember is that consciousness is a biological phenomenon like any other. It is true that it has special features, most notably the feature of subjectivity, as we have seen, but that does not prevent consciousness from being a higher-level feature of the brain in the same way that digestion is a higher-level feature of the stomach, or liquidity a higher-level feature of the system of molecules that constitute our blood. In short, the way to reply to materialism is to point out that it ignores the real existence of consciousness. The way to defeat dualism is simply to refuse to accept the system of categories that makes consciousness out as something nonbiological, not a part of the natural world.

I said that we should not think of dualism as a theory exclusive to Western philosophy. Its wider appeal is illustrated by the fact that an Eastern religious figure such as the Dalai Lama also embraces it. But though it is, so to speak, "multicultural," it is not universal. I was deeply impressed by an African friend of mine who told me that in his native African language the "mind-body problem," as we think of it, cannot even be stated. I am now trying to revise the European conceptual categories so that the problem is no longer stateable in the way that it has traditionally been presented. Grant me that consciousness, with all its subjectivity, is caused by processes in the brain, and grant me that conscious states are themselves higher-level features of the brain. Once you have granted these two propositions, there is no metaphysical mind-body problem left. The traditional problem arises only if you accept the vocabulary with its mutually exclusive categories of mental and physical, mind and matter, spirit and flesh. Of course, consciousness is still special among biological phenomena. Consciousness has a first-person ontology and so cannot be reduced to, or eliminated in favor of, phenomena with a third-person ontology. But that is just a fact about how nature works. It is a fact of neurobiology that certain brain processes cause conscious states and processes. I am urging that we should grant the facts without accepting the metaphysical baggage that traditionally goes along with the facts.

When I say that the brain is a biological organ and consciousness a biological process, I do not, of course, say or imply that it would be impossible to produce an artificial brain out of nonbiological materials that could also cause and sustain consciousness. The heart is also a biological organ, and the pumping of blood a biological process, but it is possible to build an artificial heart that pumps blood. There is no reason, in principle, why we could not similarly make an artificial brain that causes consciousness. The point that needs to be emphasized is that any such artificial brain would have to duplicate the actual causes of human and animal brains to produce inner, qualitative, subjective states of consciousness. Just producing similar output behavior would not by itself be enough.

We can summarize these points in the following propositions.

1. Consciousness consists of inner, qualitative, subjective states and processes. It has therefore a first-person ontology.

2. Because it has a first-person ontology, consciousness cannot be reduced to third-person phenomena in the way that is typical of other natural phenomena such as heat, liquidity, or solidity.

3. Consciousness is, above all, a biological phenomenon. Conscious processes are biological processes.

4. Conscious processes are caused by lower-level neuronal processes in the brain.

5. Consciousness consists of higher-level processes realized in the structure of the brain.

6. There is, as far as we know, no reason in principle why we could not build an artificial brain that also causes and realizes consciousness.

But that is it. That is our account of the metaphysical relations between consciousness and the brain. Nowhere do we even raise the questions of dualism and materialism. They have simply become obsolete categories.

We have thus "naturalized" consciousness, and indeed, my label for this view is "biological naturalism": "naturalism" because, on this view, the mind is part of nature, and "biological" because the mode of explanation of the existence of mental phenomena is biological—as opposed to, for example, computational, behavioral, social, or linguistic.

This method, I believe, is one of the ways to make progress in philosophy. When confronted with an intractable question such as is presented by a clash of convincing default positions, don't accept the question lying down. Get up and go behind the question to see what assumptions lie behind the alternatives the question presents. In this case, we did not answer the question in terms of the alternatives presented to us but we *overcame* the question. The question was, is dualism or materialism the correct analysis of the mental? The answer is: as traditionally conceived, neither; as revised, both. Hence it is best to reject the vocabulary of "dualism" and "materialism" altogether and start over. The answer is then given by propositions 1–5. The view can be summarized even more succinctly by saying: consciousness is caused by brain processes and is a higher-level feature of the brain system.

The way we proceeded was to start by reminding ourselves of what we know about how the world works. In this case, we know that consciousness consists in states and processes that are ontologically subjective, are caused by processes in the brain, and are realized in the brain. We then saw that the picture that emerged from our knowledge of the facts was inconsistent with both of the traditional alternatives presented to us, dualism and materialism. So our next step was to ask: What are both theories assuming that makes the initial question seem insoluble? And the answer is that they are assuming, as Descartes did, that the categories of mind and body, of matter and consciousness, are mutually exclusive. Our solution, then, was to get rid of those categories. In so doing, we found we could consistently accept all of the facts that we knew independently of our philosophical commitments.

The Irreducibility of Consciousness

I have said that the subjectivity of consciousness makes it irreducible to third-person phenomena, according to the standard models of scientific reduction. But why exactly? The problem can be put as follows: if, as I have been insisting, consciousness is an ordinary biological phenomenon like mitosis, meiosis, or digestion, then we ought to be able to say exactly how consciousness reduces to micro-phenomena in a way that mitosis or digestion do. Thus, for example, in the case of digestion, once you have told the entire story about the enzymes, the renin, the breakdown of the carbohydrates, and so on, there is nothing more to say. There isn't any further property of digestion in addition to that. And, of course, those processes have a further description in the behavior of even more micro-elements, such as quarks and muons, until finally we get to the most fundamental quantum phenomena. But in consciousness, the situation seems to be different, because once we have explained the causal basis of consciousness in terms of the firing of neurons in the thalamus and the various cortical layers, or, for that matter, in terms of quarks or muons, it seems we still have a phenomenon left over. In the case of consciousness, we have an irreducible subjective element left after we have given a complete causal account of the neurobiological basis. What is going on? Doesn't this force us to property dualism?

In order to answer this question, I have to say a bit more about scientific reduction. There are very many different kinds of scientific reduction, and the notion is not at all clear. For present purposes, however, we need to distinguish between two kinds of reduction that I call "eliminative" and "non-eliminative" reduction. Eliminative reductions get rid of a phenomenon by showing that it really doesn't exist, that it was just an illusion. For example, when we explain the appearance of sunrises and sunsets, there is a sense in which we eliminate sunrises and sunsets because we show they are only illusions. The sun does not really set over the mountains—rather, the rotation of the earth on its axis makes it appear that the sun sets.

This is different from the non-eliminative reduction of features such as liquidity and solidity. Solidity can be entirely explained causally in terms of the vibratory motions of molecules in lattice structures. Once the molecules are moving in this way, then objects are impenetrable by other objects. They support other objects, and so forth. Solidity is causally explainable in terms of the behavior of micro-elements, and for that reason we redefine solidity in terms of its causal basis. The reduction of solidity to the movement of molecules is a non-eliminative causal reduction. The table does not just appear to be solid, it *is* solid.

Now, and here is the point, we cannot make either of these moves with consciousness. Why not? We cannot perform eliminative reduction on consciousness because the pattern of eliminative reductions is to show that the phenomenon reduced is just an illusion. But where consciousness is concerned, the existence of the "illusion" is the reality itself. That is to say, if it seems to me that I am conscious, then I am. There isn't anything more to consciousness than a sequence of just such "seemings." In this respect, consciousness differs from sunsets because I may have the illusion of the sun setting behind the mountains when it does not really do so. But I cannot in that way have the illusion of consciousness if I am not conscious. The "illusion" of consciousness is identical with consciousness.

But why can't we perform a reduction of consciousness to its micro-physical causal basis as we can perform a reduction of, for example, solidity to its micro-physical basis? Well, I believe we could if we were willing to leave out subjectivity and just talk about its causes. We might, for example, become so medically sophisticated that we could look at a person's brain with our brain-o-scope and see that he was suffering a pain in his elbow, just because we could see that the appropriate neuron firings were going on. For scientific purposes, we might even define a pain in the elbow as a sequence of certain sorts of neuron firings occurring in such and such a place in the brain. But we leave something out in this case, something essential to our concept of consciousness. What we leave out is subjectivity. Consciousness has a first-person ontology, and we cannot for that reason perform a reduction on consciousness that we can on third-person phenomena, without leaving out its essential character. Notice that when we reduce solidity to molecule motion, we leave out the subjective experiences of people who encounter solid objects. We simply carve off the subjective experiences, because they are not essential to our concept of solidity. But we cannot carve off the subjective experiences of consciousness, because the whole point of having the concept of consciousness in the first place is to have a name for the subjective first-person phenomena. Although consciousness is a biological phenomenon like any other, its subjective, first-person ontology makes it impossible to reduce it to objective third-person phenomena in the way that we can reduce third-person phenomena such as digestion or solidity.

The Danger of Epiphenomenalism

Suppose for the sake of argument that I am right so far: consciousness is indeed caused by lower-level biological processes in the brain and is itself a higher-level feature of the brain system. Traditional philosophers, still in the grip of the dualistic categories, will immediately pose the following objection: on this view, consciousness must be epiphenomenal.

What they mean by that is that consciousness, though caused by brain processes, cannot itself cause anything. It is just a kind of vaporous residue cast off by the brain, but is unable to do anything on its own. Indeed—as the objector presses the argument more aggressively—it must follow from the account so far that consciousness is a kind of residue that doesn't function causally in producing anything. So, for example, if you raise your arm, you will think that your conscious decision caused your arm to go up, but in fact we all know that there is a detailed causal story to be told at the level of neurons in the motor cortex, neurotransmitters, especially acetylcholene, axon endplates, muscle fibers, and all the rest of the neurophysiology that is quite sufficient to give a complete causal account of the movement of your arm independent of any reference to consciousness. So, it seems that any realist account of consciousness, as I have been proposing, must render it epiphenomenal. It must render consciousness utterly useless and irrelevant to what happens in the world.

How shall we reply to epiphenomenalism? One consideration occurs immediately: it would be miraculous, unlike anything that ever occurred in biological history, if something in biology as elaborate, rich, and structured as human and animal consciousness made no causal difference to the real world. From what we know about evolution, it is unlikely that epiphenomenalism could be right. This is not a decisive objection to epiphenomenalism, but it ought at least to make us wrinkle our noses at the thought of epiphenomenalism. What, then, is the answer? Once again, let's go behind the question and ask: What is being presupposed by the challenge of epiphenomenalism?

The standard model of causation, the earliest experience of causes that the child gets, and the most primitive concept of causation we have, is the notion of one object exerting a physical pressure on another. Piaget's researches on the early development of children show that the child's most primitive concept of causation is a "push-pull" concept.[3] One object pushes against another, and the child pushes and pulls against objects. This is how the child acquires his or her most basic concept of causation. As the child comes to understand more about how the world works—and more important, as we come to understand scientifically how the world works— we get a much more expanded and richer conception of causal relations. We can then see that causation is in general a matter of one thing making something else happen, and thus we can talk not only about the causes of buildings collapsing but about the causes of wars and economic depressions, the causes of mental illness and changes in popular culture. Causation, in short, is not just a matter of pushing and pulling, it is a matter of something being responsible for something else happening.

Let us think for a moment about how consciousness works in real life to make things happen. I consciously raise my arm, and my conscious effort causes my arm to go up. My *conscious* effort actually produces a change in the position of my arm. Prereflectively we do not doubt that this happens in real life. When we begin to have skeptical philosophical doubts about how it *could* happen, about how the experienced causal relation can be made consistent with our "scientific worldview," I believe that we are combining our residual dualism with an extremely naive conception of causal relations. If we start with push-pull, billiard-ball causation, it will seem puzzling that mental states can cause physical changes. It will seem even more puzzling if we think with the dualists that the "mental" is not part of the "physical" world.

But suppose we reject both of these assumptions. Suppose we start with what we independently know. *Suppose we start with the fact that the mind affects the body and the body affects the mind, and go from there.* That is, let us assume at the start what we all know from our own experiences—that there are causal relations between consciousness and other physical events. For example, when I consciously intend to raise my arm, my conscious state causes my arm to go up; when I bump into a solid object, the impact of the object causes me to feel a sensation of pain. Let us start, at least provisionally, with an acceptance of these facts and then redraw the conceptual map so that it accurately reflects them.

This redrawing of the conceptual map to reflect the facts is typical of the growth of philosophical and scientific understanding. An early objection to Newtonian mechanics was that gravitation as a causal force seemed to imply "action at a distance." To avoid the absurdity of action at a distance, we seemed to be forced to think of gravitation as a matter of invisible strings tying planetary bodies together. Today nobody makes this sort of objection. We have a much richer conception of causation, which includes, among other things, fields of force. We no longer suppose that in order for one planet to act causally on another there must be a physical object connecting the two, so that they can push or pull one another.

But once again, the objector will ask, "How is it possible that the mind can affect the body?" That is, the objector will complain that it is not enough for me to keep roundly insisting that intuitively we feel that epiphenomenalism is false. Can there be any grounds for this feeling? What is the conceptual map supposed to look like when we have redrawn it in such a way as to make mind-body causation possible?

Our first step was to remove the assumption that all causation is a case of something pushing or pulling something else. Not all causation is billiard-ball causation. The second and final step is to remind ourselves of how causation works in physical systems anyway. If you think of the behavior of your car engine, for example, you will see that there are different causally real levels of description. At one level, we talk about the action of the piston, the cylinders, the spark plugs, and the explosion in the cylinder. At a lower level, we can talk about the passage of electrons across the electrodes, the oxidization of hydrocarbons, the molecular structure of the metal alloys, and the formation of new compounds such as

CO and CO_2. These are two quite distinct levels of description of the behavior of an engine, but there is nothing inconsistent between these two descriptions, and there is no reason to regard the higher-level description as epiphenomenal or causally unreal. Of course, everything in nature has to bottom out at the most basic level—the level of quarks and muons and subatomic particles. The fact that any given causal level is grounded in more fundamental levels until finally we reach the basic level of the micro-particles does not show that the higher level is not causally real. In short, the argument for the epiphenomenalism of the mental is no stronger than for the epiphenomenalism of pistons and cylinders. The fact that you can give a causal account at the lower level does not imply that the higher levels are not real. That is, our provisional acceptance of the causal efficacy of consciousness is not threatened by pointing out that any explanation at the level of consciousness is grounded in more fundamental physical phenomena, because it is true of any physical system whatever that causal explanations at the higher levels are grounded in more fundamental micro-physical explanations at the lower levels. It does not prove that the solidity of the piston is epiphenomenal to point out that solidity is explainable in terms of the molecular behavior of the alloys; similarly, it does not prove that intentions are epiphenomenal to point out that intentions are explainable in terms of neurons, synapses, and neurotransmitters.

To summarize our reply to epiphenomenalism, we can say that three mistakes underlie the epiphenomenalist argument.

1. The dualistic assumption that the mental is not part of the physical world
2. The assumption that all causation must be on the model of physical objects pushing against other physical objects—billiard-ball causation
3. The assumption that for any causal level, if you can give an account of the functioning of that level in terms of more basic micro-structures, then the initial

level was causally unreal, epiphenomenal—not effica-
cious

I believe all three of these assumptions are unjustified, indeed false, and once their falsity has been pointed out, I believe there is no ground for saying that consciousness is
epiphenomenal.

I want to make my position absolutely clear here. I am not
saying that it is a matter of logic that epiphenomenalism is
false. As far as logical possibility is concerned, it might turn
out that mental states are totally epiphenomenal and thus do
not play any causal role. Such a possibility is logically conceivable, but as far as we know, it is just a plain fact about
how the world works that our conscious mental states function causally in the production of our behavior. The world
might have turned out differently, but this is how it turned
out in fact. I have tried to remove the grounds for doubting
this fact. I have tried to remove the grounds for thinking that
consciousness must be epiphenomenal, but I have not proved
that epiphenomenalism is logically absurd. I believe it is
false, but the form of falsity in question is empirical falsity,
not logical absurdity. If epiphenomenalism did turn out to be
true, it would be the greatest scientific revolution in the history of the world and would alter our whole way of thinking
about reality. My aim here was to remove the reasons for
thinking that epiphenomenalism must be true.

The Function of Consciousness

This raises the question, what is the evolutionary function of
consciousness? What is its evolutionary value? What does it
do? What good is it for survival?

This question is sometimes asked in a polemical, rhetorical tone, as if to suggest that maybe consciousness doesn't
matter, that maybe it is just going along for a free ride, and

that we could just as well have evolved without it. This is a very strange suggestion to make, because much of what we do that is essential to the survival of our species requires consciousness: you cannot eat, copulate, raise your young, hunt for food, raise crops, speak a language, organize social groups, or heal the sick if you are in a coma. The polemical suggestion is that somehow or other we could imagine beings like ourselves having evolved ways of doing these things without consciousness.

Well, we can imagine any science fiction fantasy we like. But in the real world, the way that humans and higher animals typically cope is by way of conscious activities. We can imagine plants producing food by some method other than photosynthesis, but this does not show that photosynthesis has no function in evolution. In the real world, plants need photosynthesis, and humans need consciousness, in order to survive.

There is something extremely puzzling about the claim that consciousness plays no evolutionary role, because it is obvious that consciousness plays a large number of such roles. The skeptics on this issue I believe are still tacitly assuming a dualism of mind and body when they make the skeptical challenge. Here is how. The normal way we have of inquiring into the evolutionary role of some phenotypical trait is to imagine the absence of that trait, *while holding the rest of nature constant*, and then see what happens. When you imagine that plants could not perform photosynthesis or that birds could not fly, holding the rest of nature constant, you can see the evolutionary advantage of these traits. Now try it with consciousness. Imagine that we all fall into a coma and lie around prostrate and helpless. You see that we would soon become extinct, but that is not the way the skeptic imagines it. He imagines that our behavior remains the same, only minus consciousness. But that is precisely *not* holding the rest of nature constant, because in real life much of the behavior that enables us to survive is conscious behavior. In real life you cannot subtract the consciousness and keep the behavior. To suppose you can is to suppose that consciousness is not an ordinary physical part of the physical world. That is, it is to suppose a dualistic account of consciousness. Skepticism about the evolutionary role of consciousness thus presupposes that consciousness is not already an ordinary part of the physical biological world that we all live in.

Consciousness, Intentionality, and Causation

I have been talking as if consciousness functioned causally, so to speak, just like that. The way an explosion knocks over a building, for example. But typically a conscious state such as an intention or a desire functions by representing the sort of event that it causes. For example, I want to drink water, so I drink water. Here the effect, drinking water, is consciously represented by the cause, the desire to drink water. This sort of mental causation I call "intentional causation," for reasons that emerge in chapter 4. At this point, I just want to remark on the amazing property that conscious beings have to represent objects and states of affairs in the world and *to act on the basis of those representations*. It is a general feature of most, though not all, conscious phenomena that they represent objects, events, and states of affairs in the world. Indeed, the most important feature of consciousness for the purpose of this discussion is that there is an essential connection between consciousness and the capacity that we human beings have to represent objects and states of affairs in the world to ourselves. This is a feature possessed by beliefs and desires, hopes and fears, love and hate, pride and shame, as well as perception and intention. It is a feature that has a technical name in philosophy: "intentionality." Intentionality is that feature of the mind by which mental states are directed at, or are about or of, or refer to, or aim at, states of affairs in the world. It is a peculiar feature in that the object need not actually exist in order to be represented by our intentional state. Thus, the child can believe that Santa Claus will come on Christmas Eve, even though Santa Claus doesn't exist.

Not all conscious states are intentional, and not all intentional states are conscious. Thus, for example, there are conscious feelings of anxiety or elation for which there is no answer to the question, "What are you anxious about or what are you elated about?" These are non-intentional forms of consciousness. And of course, there are many forms of intentionality that are not conscious. I have beliefs and desires, hopes and fears, even when I am sound asleep. It is true to say of me that I believe that Bill Clinton is president of the United State even at times when I am totally unconscious. But that belief then exists in an unconscious form. It still has its intentionality, but it is no longer conscious.

Nonetheless, though not all conscious states are intentional, and not all intentional states are conscious, there is an essential connection: we only understand intentionality in terms of consciousness. There are many intentional states that are not conscious, but they are the sort of thing that could potentially be conscious.

In the next two chapters, we explore the structure of consciousness and the structure of intentionality.

THREE

The Essence of the Mind: Consciousness and Its Structure

Naively, one might suppose consciousness would be the best understood of any phenomenon. After all, are we not in direct contact with our own consciousness throughout our waking and dreaming lives, and what could be easier than simply giving a description of our own conscious experiences? However, it turns out not to be so easy. If you try to describe your consciousness, you find that in large part what you do is describe the objects and events in your immediate vicinity. After describing your inner body sensations, moods, emotions, and thoughts, you describe the contents of your consciousness by describing things that you consciously perceive. If you look around the room and see chairs and tables, there isn't anything to describe by way of describing your consciousness except the chairs and tables that you see and the impression they make on you. Even if you describe your conscious thoughts about objects that are not present or events that occurred in the past, most of what you have to say about your conscious states will still be about those absent objects or past events. Part of the difficulty in getting a description of consciousness is that it does not seem to be itself an object of observation in the way that other things, such as the chairs and tables in your vicinity, are objects of observation.

The first difficulty in getting an account of consciousness arises out of the peculiar relation in which consciousness stands to observation. We cannot observe consciousness in the way that we can observe mountains and oceans because the only candidate for observation is the act of observing itself. We cannot make the distinction between the observation and the thing observed for consciousness itself, as we can for other targets of observation. This point has important consequences for the doctrine of introspection, as we will see.

A second difficulty is that we have inherited a long philosophical tradition that refuses to treat consciousness as part of the ordinary, natural, "physical" world that we all live in. Consciousness is treated as something mysterious, something to the side of the world, or above it, something apart from the rest of nature, but not a part of the ordinary physical world. On the one hand, dualists treat consciousness as a metaphysically distinct, nonphysical phenomenon. On the other hand, materialists deny its existence as a real and irreducible phenomenon and maintain that there really is no such thing as consciousness over and above "material" or "physical" processes described in third-person terms. My position, as I explained in chapter 2, is neither of these. My insistence that consciousness is an irreducible phenomenon will make my position sound like property dualism, but my simultaneous insistence that consciousness is an ordinary biological phenomenon like digestion or photosynthesis will make my position sound like materialism. Perhaps not surprisingly, I have been characterized by some of my commentators as a materialist and by others as a dualist. The way out of this clash of default positions, as is often the case in philosophy, is to make a *conceptual* revision. The problem is not with our access to the facts. The problem is with the set of categories that we have inherited for describing the facts. On the one hand, we have the model of scientific knowledge that is knowledge of the "physical world," and we have inherited a philosophical tradition that says that consciousness is not a part of the physical world. The way out, as we saw in chapter 2, is to abandon the set of categories—specifically, to abandon the notion that "mental" and "physical" name mutually exclusive classes. Once we see that consciousness is a biological phenomenon like any other, then we can see that, of course, in some sense it is completely "material." It is part of our biology. On the other hand, consciousness is not reducible to any process that consists of physical phenomena describable exclusively in third-person physical terms. Therefore, it looks like we have to reject materialism. The solution is not to deny any of the obvious facts, but to shift the categories around so we recognize that consciousness is at one and the same time completely material and irreducibly mental. And that means we should simply abandon the traditional categories of "material" and "mental" as they have been used in the Cartesian tradition.

Three Mistakes About Consciousness

Before trying to describe the structure of consciousness, I want to begin by exposing and correcting several standard mistakes about the nature of consciousness that are commonly made in our philosophical tradition and almost appear to be endemic to our philosophical culture.

First, the fact that consciousness has a subjective mode of existence has led many people to suppose that we must have a special kind of certainty when it comes to knowing our own conscious states. Descartes famously argued that we have absolute certainty about our conscious states. We cannot be mistaken in our claims about them, and for that reason, our claims about them are said to be "incorrigible," meaning that they cannot be corrected by further evidence. This seems to me to be a mistake. There is indeed an asymmetry, as I pointed out earlier, between the way I have access to my conscious states and the way that you have access to my conscious states. But this does not imply that I cannot be mistaken about my conscious states. On the contrary, it seems to me that people often make mistaken judgments about their own conscious states. They deny that they are jealous when it is obvious to any observer that in fact they are jealous. They say that they have a firm intention to do something when, again, it is obvious to any outside observer that they lack any such intention. How is it possible that we can be mistaken about our own conscious states? There are several different dimensions in which we can make such a mistake, and I will briefly mention four of these.

The first way that we can be wrong about our own conscious states is by self-deception. We simply deceive ourselves about our own mental states because it is too painful to confront our jealousies, hostilities, weaknesses, and so on. We refuse to admit, even to ourselves, our most shameful feelings and attitudes.

It is easy to give a philosophical "proof" that self-deception is impossible, but since we all know it *is* possible, there must be something wrong with the proof. Here is the proof: In order for A to deceive B about a proposition p, A must believe that p and deliberately induce in B a belief that *not p*. But where A = B this is impossible because A would have to end up believing both p and *not p*, which is a contradiction. The answer to this proof, and the resolution of the paradox, is to point out that self-deception requires unconscious mental processes. You can consciously believe and sincerely claim that you intend to give up smoking while in fact unconsciously knowing that you have no such intention. Such is the nature of self-deception. Thus, you consciously claim that p while unconsciously knowing that $not\ p$, and even resisting bringing that knowledge of $not\ p$ to your consciousness.

Related to self-deception, and a second source of errors about our own conscious states, is misinterpretation. For example, in a moment of great emotion you might sincerely think that you are in love, but later you realize that you had misinterpreted your feelings and the emotion was only a temporary infatuation.

A third, and I believe the most common, source of error about our own mental states is related to the second. Many of our mental states are conceptually tied to our behavior under certain descriptions. Thus, if I say I have a firm and unconditional intention to do something, then unless I exhibit at least some disposition to do the thing I purportedly intend to do, we may reasonably doubt that I made a correct attribution of an intention to myself. It is, in short, a mistake to suppose that there is a clean separation between the verbal categories that apply to consciousness and those that apply to subsequent behavior. Many important mental concepts, such as intending, deciding, or performing actions, in fact straddle the categories of the conscious states and subsequent behavior. We think, for example, that we have really made up our minds to stop smoking, lose weight, work harder, or write a book, but our subsequent behavior proves we were wrong.

If I am intentionally performing the action of writing a book, then of course that is a conscious activity, but unlike the mere thought of writing a book, it has all sorts of physical aspects. In order to be writing a book, I actually have to do something. My body has to move in certain sorts of ways if I am to be writing a book.

A fourth form of mistake about our own conscious states is inattention—we simply don't pay close enough attention to the ways in which our consciousness is proceeding. We think, for example, that we are firmly committed to a certain political stance, but over the years we discover that without our even noticing it, our political preferences have changed.

So it is a mistake to suppose that our knowledge of our own conscious states is certain and incorrigible.

A second mistake we tend to make about consciousness in our philosophical tradition, related to the mistake about incorrigibility, is the view that our conscious states are known by a special faculty—a kind of inner mental vision—called "introspection." As suggested by the morphology of the word, we are supposed to understand introspection using the model of vision. We think of knowing our conscious states by a special inner eye. We "spect intro," that is, we turn the inner eye of our "spective" capacities "intro" into our own conscious states in order to observe them. This also seems to me to be a mistake, and the reason it is a mistake can be stated quite simply. The model of vision requires a distinction between the act of perceiving and the object perceived. If I see this chair, then in the act of perception, there is a distinction between the chair and the experience of perceiving in which I perceive the chair. But we cannot make these distinctions for experiences themselves. For example, if I perceive my pain, I cannot distinguish between the pain and the perception of the pain. In other words, I cannot make the distinction that would make the model of vision work, the distinction between the experience of perceiving and the object perceived. For that reason, it seems to be mistaken to suppose that the right way to understand our conscious states and how we know them is on the model of vision via a special faculty of inner perception called "introspection."

The third common mistake in our philosophical tradition about consciousness, and perhaps the most subtle mistake of all, is the doctrine that all of our states of consciousness involve *self-consciousness*. There are two ways of interpreting the doctrine that all conscious states are self-conscious, and both of them seem to me false. The first interpretation is that whenever I am conscious of anything, I am conscious of myself being conscious of that thing. This seems to me mistaken as a matter of fact. I am often, in thinking about something, simply thinking about it and not thinking about myself thinking about it. It is not the case that all conscious states have to have a second-order awareness of the agent having the conscious state. A different, and really quite distinct, interpretation of the doctrine of self-consciousness is that all conscious states have themselves as an intentional object. The theory is that, for example, as I look out the window and survey the view of the Pacific Ocean, I must have as part of the object of my perception the actual perception itself. I must have a second-order awareness of the perception in addition to my awareness of the objects perceived. This also seems to me a mistake. There are indeed cases where I focus my attention on the act of perceiving and not on the object perceived. The impressionist painters are often said to have focused their attention on the experiences they had of objects rather than on the objects themselves when they painted. Such cases do indeed occur, but it is not part of the definition—part of the very concept of conscious perception—that self-consciousness of this sort should occur in every case.

Structural Features of Consciousness

So far the argument of this chapter must seem mainly negative. I have been mostly concerned to say a lot about what consciousness is not. Now I want to state some of the things that consciousness is. Perhaps the best way is simply to list important features of consciousness, and I will, for the sake of brevity, confine myself to the ten most salient.

1. The most important feature of consciousness, the one that I have already called attention to, is *ontological subjectivity*. All conscious states only exist as experienced by an agent. This is the feature that philosophers have been driving at for

generations when they tried to describe the special character of consciousness. It is this feature of consciousness that has led many materialist philosophers to want to deny the existence of consciousness, in the most ordinary sense of the word, and that has made it exceptionally hard to assimilate consciousness into our overall scientific worldview.

2. A second feature is absolutely crucial to understanding consciousness: consciousness comes to us in a *unified form*. I don't just perceive the pressure of the shoes on my feet, the thought of a philosophical problem, the sound of the traffic in the background, and the sight of the hills beyond, but I have all of these experiences as part of one unified, single experience. The ability to bind together all of the diverse stimuli that come into my body by way of the sensory nerve endings and unite them into a unified, coherent perceptual experience is a remarkable capacity of the brain, and at present we do not know how the brain does it. From a neurobiological point of view, it is a remarkable fact that the enormous variety of stimulus inputs that the brain receives—the stimulation of the optical system by the assault of photons on the photoreceptor cells when I see something, and of the peripheral nerve endings of the somatosensory system when I touch an object, the stimulation of the olfactory and auditory systems by external irritation—are converted into a single, unified conscious experience. This unity, more than anything else, refutes the view that there really are different kinds of consciousness, or different senses of the word *consciousness*. There is indeed a distinction between thinking and feeling, but the remarkable thing about consciousness is that thinking and feeling go on at the same time in the same field of consciousness. I am now thinking about philosophical problems and simultaneously feeling a mild pain in my toe. It is true that these are two different conscious states, but they are both part of a single, united field of consciousness—of one total conscious experience.

It seems to me that the unity of consciousness comes in two forms. First, there is what we might call "vertical" unity: all of our conscious states are united at any given instant into a single, unified conscious field. But across time, the preservation of a unity of our experiences requires at least a minimal short-term memory. I couldn't have the consciousness of a coherent thought unless both a beginning and an ending of the thought were part of a single, unified field of consciousness united by memory. To put this point bluntly, without memory, there is no organized consciousness. We might call this feature "horizontal" unity as opposed to vertical unity. If we think of time as moving from left to right horizontally, then the metaphor enables us to see that this is a different sort of unity from the instantaneous vertical unity of our conscious field.

One of the best ways to study consciousness is to study its breakdowns, to study its pathologies. And we have found breakdowns in both the horizontal and vertical dimensions. The split-brain patients exhibit a breakdown in vertical unity. The patients with brain defects that produce deficits in short-term and iconic memories illustrate breakdowns of horizontal unity.

The split-brain patients are the most spectacular examples of breakdowns in unified consciousness. In these cases, patients with severe forms of epilepsy have had the corpus colossum, a body of tissue that connects the two halves of the brain, severed. The result is that they appear to have two independent loci of consciousness, and these communicate with each other only imperfectly. Thus, in a typical experiment, a split-brain patient has a spoon shown to his left eye, which connects to the right side of his brain. He is then asked, "What do you see?" His language ability is on the left side of his brain, and with the left side of his brain, he answers sincerely, "I don't see anything." Then with his left hand, which is controlled by the right side of his brain, which is in fact seeing a spoon, he reaches out and grabs the spoon. We now have a very large number of these cases, so there is no doubt about the validity of the clinical data.[1] These patients exhibit a breakdown in vertical unity.

There have also been many experiments that showed that patients with certain sorts of brain damage cannot have an ordered sequence of conscious states because they have lost the capacity to organize their experiences by way of memory. A typical example is that of a patient suffering from Korsakov's syndrome, who is introduced to a doctor and has a brief conversation with him. The doctor then leaves the room, and when he reenters a few moments later, the patient does not recognize him. The patient's memory is insufficient to organize the ongoing sequence of his conscious states.[2]

I will say more about the unity of the field of consciousness in the next section.

3. The feature of consciousness that is most essential for our survival in the world is that consciousness gives us access to the world other than our own conscious states. The two modes in which it does this are the cognitive mode, where we represent how things are, and the volitive or conative mode, in which we represent how we want them to be, or how we are trying to make them become. I discuss these modes in more detail in the next chapter, but at present I just want to call attention to the fact that consciousness is essentially tied to *intentionality*. There are many unconscious intentional states and many conscious states that are not intentional, but there is an essential connection between consciousness and intentionality in this crucial respect: the attribution of a mental state to an agent is either an attribution of a conscious state or an attribution of a state that is the sort of thing that could be conscious. So, for example, if I say of Jones, "Jones believes that Clinton is president of the United States," I can say this even when Jones is sound asleep. But what I am attributing to him here and now is not a conscious belief here and now that Clinton is president, but rather a brain capacity that enables him to have the conscious belief that Clinton is president. There are plenty of "unconscious mental states," but an unconscious state is *mental* only in virtue of its capacity in principle to produce a conscious mental state. I have to say "in principle" because an unconscious state may *in fact* be inaccessible to consciousness because of brain damage, repression, or other causes. But such states must be the sort of thing that can be conscious.

4. An important feature of consciousness, it seems to me, is that all of our conscious states come to us in one *mood* or another. We are always in some mood, even if it does not have a name like "elation" or "depression." Right now, for example, I am not especially elated, or especially depressed; indeed, I am not even just "blah." Nonetheless, there is what one might call a certain flavor to my experiences. This flavor is what I mean by mood. Any conscious state you may have always comes with some sort of coloration. This fact becomes clear during a dramatic shift. If I suddenly receive some very bad news that sends me into a state of depression, or I receive some extremely good news that sends me into a state of elation, I become acutely aware of the shift in my mood.

5. The fifth feature of conscious states is that in their non-pathological forms they are always *structured*. The most dramatic examples of this come from the gestalt psychologists. They showed, among many other things, that the brain will structure even very degenerate stimulus input into a coherent figure. This is obvious in the case of vision, but I think it is true of the other perceptual modalities as well, and true of consciousness in general—that we structure our conscious experiences into coherent wholes.

Consider the following example:

The actual lines on the page do not really look like a human face, but the brain structures the stimulus input so that you *see them as* a human face.

There are really two aspects of the gestalt structure. In one aspect, we structure our experiences into wholes, but in the other, we always have our experiences of any intentional object as a figure against the background. So, for example, I now see the book against the background of the desk. I see the desk against the background of the floor, the floor against the background of the room, until I reach the horizon of my conscious experiences.

6. The sixth feature of consciousness is that it comes in varying degrees of *attention*. In any conscious experience, we need to distinguish the center from the periphery of our attention within the field of consciousness, and typically we are able to shift our attention at will. For example, I can now pay attention to the computer screen in front of me and ignore the pressure of my body against the chair. I am not, strictly speaking, *unconscious* of the pressure of my body against the chair, it is just that it is on the periphery of my consciousness. The fact that peripheral consciousness is not the same as unconsciousness is shown by the fact that I can shift my attention away from the computer screen to the pressure of my body on the chair, thus bringing what was on the periphery to the center. The metaphor of the searchlight is almost irresistible here. Attention is like a light that I can shift from one part of my conscious field to another.

7. A seventh feature of our conscious states, related to but not identical with the distinction between the center and the periphery created by our varying degrees of attention, is that conscious states typically come with a *sense of their own situatedness*. I call this feature the *boundary conditions* of consciousness. Each of our conscious states comes with a sense of our own location in space and time even though the location itself is not an intentional object of our consciousness. So, for example, I am typically aware of what time of year it is, of what country and what city I am in, of whether or not it is after breakfast or after dinner. I am similarly aware of who I am and what country I am a citizen of.

And again, as with so many features of consciousness, perhaps the most obvious way of studying the boundary conditions of consciousness is to look at the pathological examples. In some forms of almost vertiginous disorientation, one suddenly doesn't remember what month it is, or where one is.

8. The next feature of our conscious experiences is that they come to us in varying degrees of *familiarity*. We experience things on a continuum, on a spectrum, that goes from the most familiar to the most strange. When I enter my room, I experience the objects in the room as familiar objects. Indeed, even when I am in what is to me an extremely strange environment, such as a jungle or a village in a remote part of the world, still, however strange the houses and the people may look to me, those are still houses, they are still dwelling places, and the people are still people. Surrealist painters try to break this sense of familiarity, but even in the surrealist painting the three-headed woman is still a woman and the drooping watch is still a watch. It is very hard to break the aspect of familiarity of our conscious experiences, and this follows from the facts of intentionality, namely, that all mental representation is under an aspect. The aspects under which we perceive things as being houses, chairs, people, cars, and so forth, are aspects with which we are familiar. Familiarity is a scalar phenomenon. Things are experienced by us as more or less familiar.

9. It is characteristic of our conscious experiences that they typically refer beyond themselves. We never just have an isolated experience, but it always spins out to further experiences beyond. Each thought we have reminds us of other thoughts. Each sight we see carries reference to things unseen. I call this feature *overflow*. As I look out of my window right now, I see houses and people, and I see them in the context of my previous experience. I am immediately set on a train of thought as to who these people are, how these houses remind me of other houses I have seen, and other thoughts flow from that.

10. Conscious states are always *pleasurable or unpleasurable* to some degree. For any conscious experience, there is always a question: Did you enjoy it? Was it fun? Were you happy, unhappy, bored, amused, entertained, exasperated, furious, pleased, disgusted, or simply indifferent? Like familiarity, the pleasurable-unpleasurable dimension is a scalar dimension. Conscious experiences range in differing degrees of pleasantness and unpleasantness, and of course, one and the same conscious experience can contain both pleasant and unpleasant aspects.

The Field of Consciousness and the Binding Problem

I have throughout this chapter been talking as if at any given point the totality of one's consciousness is made up of the various bits within it. This way of thinking, where we think of a totality as composed of its elements, is so useful and natural to us in dealing with other problems that we are unaware of the extent to which it may be inappropriate where consciousness is concerned. If you think of consciousness, for example, your present conscious field, as made up of the various elements—your perception of the chair over there, your feeling of the clothing against your back, the sight of the trees and the sky outside your window, the sound of the stream coming in from below—then you are confronted with a number of serious problems. Most famously, you are confronted with the problem I mentioned in the previous section of how the brain can bind all of these various elements together into a single united conscious experience. This problem, known in neurobiology as the "binding problem," has been mostly discussed with regard to vision. How does the visual system, which has elements specialized for color, line, angle, and so on, bind all of these disparate inputs into a unified visual experience of an object such as the table in front of me? But the problem is more general, and it goes back to Kant, who correctly saw that it is a problem for consciousness in general, and indeed Kant gave the phenomenon the unattractive name of "the transcendental unity of apperception."

But maybe in current discussions of the binding problem we are thinking about consciousness in the wrong way. There is no good reason to suppose that the unity of consciousness is a matter of combining elements, that consciousness is put together like a car or a house from a lot of separate components. Let us try a different approach. Instead of starting with my present state of fully aware alert consciousness, imagine that I gradually wake up in a dark soundless room. Suppose that I gradually reach a state in which I am fully awake but I have no perceptual experiences whatever. The room is in total darkness, and there is no sound. I am not tasting or smelling anything. I can, if I concentrate my attention, focus on the weight of my body against the bed, and the proprioception of my various body parts. But aside from that, my consciousness consists in a conscious field filled only with a sequence of my conscious thoughts. Now, for such a consciousness, there does not seem to be a binding problem in quite the same way as there was before. Think of my consciousness as coming to me as an empty field, and there isn't any question about binding its various elements together. It comes, so to speak, already bound; the binding is for free. Now, as I get up and begin to move around, turn on the lights, the radio, brush my teeth, and so on, it is tempting to think that onto this field various experiences have begun to appear. And the theater metaphor is almost unavoidable. We find ourselves thinking of consciousness as a kind of stage or proscenium on which the various characters appear as elements of the consciousness. But, once again, I think that is not quite the right way to think of it. To begin with, the homunculus fallacy—the fallacy of supposing that all of my experiences are had by a little person in my head—is almost unavoidable if we think of our consciousness as a stage on which the various experiences appear, because who would be perceiving the actors on the stage other than a homunculus?

Let us try to pursue the field metaphor more closely. If we think of my consciousness as like an open prairie, then the changes in my conscious states will be more like bumps and mounds appearing on the prairie. Shifts and changes in the structure of the field, I think, are the correct metaphors for understanding the flux of our conscious experiences. Now, if we think of consciousness in this way as a vast field, and think of the particular percepts, thoughts, experiences, and so on, as variations and modifications in the structure of the field, then we do not have quite the same binding problem that we had before. There isn't any question how consciousness is unified. It is unified from the start by definition. Nothing would be conscious if it were not part of a unified field of consciousness. So, there are not two questions—how does the brain cause consciousness, and how is it unified?—but only one. An answer to the question, how the brain causes consciousness, is already an answer to the question, how it produces a unified consciousness.

We still have the binding problem for particular perceptual modalities. How do the various different perceptual inputs hang together as the experience of a particular object? But there is no longer any overall binding problem for the structure of consciousness in general because consciousness comes to us unified by definition.

We can understand this point even better if we go back to the split-brain patients. If we think of the split-brain patients as having two centers of consciousness, then we are not thinking of a single consciousness that is broken in two, we are thinking, rather, of two separate unified conscious fields. What is unthinkable is that there should be an element of consciousness that is disunified. That is, it is unthinkable that my conscious states should come to me as a simultaneous series of discrete bits, for if all of the bits were part of my conscious awareness at once, then they would all be part of a single conscious field. If, on the other hand, we were to think, for example, of seventeen bits, each as having a separate existence, then what we are thinking of is seventeen separate consciousnesses, not one consciousness with seventeen elements. My conclusion then is that the field metaphor is a better one for describing the structure of consciousness than the "putting together of bits" metaphor, which has worked so well in other areas of scientific and philosophical analysis.

Consciousness and Value

Any attempt to describe consciousness, any attempt to show how consciousness fits into the world at large, always seems to me inadequate. What we are leaving out is that consciousness is not just an important feature of reality. There is a sense in which it is *the* most important feature of reality because all other things have value, importance, merit, or worth only in relation to consciousness. If we value life, justice, beauty, survival, reproduction, it is only as conscious beings that we value them. In public discussions, I am frequently challenged to say why I think consciousness is important; any answer one can give is always pathetically inadequate because everything that is important is important in relation to consciousness. As far as coping with the world is concerned, the important feature of consciousness is that it is essentially connected to intentionality, and in the next chapter we turn to the structure of intentionality.

≡ FOUR

How the Mind Works: Intentionality

So far most of our discussion of the mind has concentrated on consciousness, and this concentration might give the impression that the mind is essentially a self-enclosed arena of subjectivity. But, on the contrary, the primary evolutionary role of the mind is to relate us in certain ways to the environment, and especially to other people. My subjective states relate me to the rest of the world, and the general name of that relationship is "intentionality." These subjective states include beliefs and desires, intentions and perceptions, as well as loves and hates, fears and hopes. "Intentionality," to repeat, is the general term for all the various forms by which the mind can be directed at, or be about, or of, objects and states of affairs in the world.

Intentionality is an unfortunate word, and like a lot of unfortunate words in philosophy, we owe it to the German-speaking philosophers. The word suggests that intentionality, in the sense of directedness, must always have some connection with "intending" in the sense in which, for example, I intend to go to the movies tonight. (German has no problem with this because *Intentionalität* does not sound like *Absicht*, the word for intention in the ordinary sense of intending to go to the movies.) So we have to keep in mind that in English intending is just one form of intentionality among many.

Consciousness and Intentionality

What is the relation between consciousness and intentionality? I mentioned in the last chapter that not all intentional states are conscious, and not all conscious states are intentional. But the overlap between consciousness and intentionality is not accidental. The relation is this: brain states that are nonconscious can be understood as *mental* states only to the extent that we understand them as capable, in principle, of giving rise to conscious states. My belief, for example, that Clinton is president of the United States can be either conscious or unconscious. I can, for example, be truly said to have that belief even when I am sound asleep. But what fact corresponds to that claim when I am totally unconscious? The only actually existing facts then and there are facts involving states of my brain that are describable in purely neurobiological terms. So what fact about those states makes them my unconscious belief that Clinton is president? The only fact that could make them into a mental state is that they are in principle capable of causing that state in a conscious form. Even when unconscious, the unconscious mental state is the sort of thing that could be conscious. I have to say "in principle" because we need to recognize that there are all sorts of states that the person cannot bring to consciousness because of repression, brain injuries, and so on. But if a state is a genuine unconscious *mental* state, then it must be at least the sort of state that could be conscious. We need, therefore, to distinguish *nonconscious* states of the brain, such as the secretion of the neurotransmitter norepenephrine into the synaptic cleft, from *unconscious* mental states that are realized in the brain—such as my belief, when I am asleep, that Clinton is president. Now, since when I am totally unconscious the only occurrent reality of the brain is nonconscious, what fact about those nonconscious states makes some of them into mental states? The only answer is that certain nonconscious states of the brain are capable of causing conscious mental phenomena.

An analogy will help make this point clear. When I turn my computer off, all of the words and images on the screen disappear. But unless I have made some terrible mistake, they do not cease to exist. Rather, they continue to be stored on the computer disk in the form of magnetic traces. What fact about those magnetic traces makes them into words and pictures? Right then and there, they are not in the form of words and pictures. Even with a powerful magnifying glass I cannot see words and pictures on the hard disk. The fact that they are still words and pictures is constituted by the fact that the magnetic traces can be converted into words and pictures when the machine is turned on. This remains true even when in fact I cannot make the conversion because the CPU is broken or some such. The computer is not like a filing cabinet, in spite of the frequent use of the filing cabinet metaphor to describe computers. When I put my texts and pictures in my filing cabinet, they retain exactly their original form. But our unconscious mental states are not like the words and pictures in the filing cabinet, still in their pristine original form; rather, they are like the words and pictures in the computer when they are not on the screen. Such mental states have a totally different, nonmental, nonconscious form, but they are still unconscious *mental* states, capable of acting causally in ways similar to conscious mental states, even though at the particular time they are unconscious there is nothing there except neurobiological states and processes describable in purely neurobiological terms.

This conception of the unconscious runs counter to the prevailing views in cognitive science. Chomsky, for example, believes that when children learn a natural human language, they do so because they are following a set of unconscious rules of Universal Grammar, but these rules are not the sorts of things that a child might bring to consciousness. The rules are "computational" rules of Universal Grammar. The linguist might formulate the rule in a technical vocabulary. The linguist might say the child follows the rule "Move alpha," but the child is not thereby assumed to be quietly thinking to himself or herself, "Move alpha." Indeed, the child is not even assumed to have the capacity to think "Move alpha." No, the formulation "Move alpha" is the linguist's way of representing processes in the brain that neither the child nor anyone else could bring to consciousness. What is going on in the child's brain is purely computational, a sequence of zeroes and ones; or some neuronal functional equivalent of zeroes and ones is being processed in the brain. But the processes are not the sort of thing that could ever be brought to consciousness.

I think the view that we have unconscious mental states that causally explain our behavior, states that are mental and yet not the sort of state that could function consciously, is incoherent. The view is incoherent because it cannot answer the question: What fact about these brain processes makes them *mental*, makes them have the features of intentional mental states? What's the difference between those nonconscious brain processes that are not mental at all and genuine unconscious mental states that, when unconscious, are states of the brain? In short, an unconscious mental state has to be *consciously thinkable* if it is to be a mental state at all as opposed to being a nonconscious brain process.

This point is terribly important for the explanation of human cognition. Genuine mental states do indeed function causally both when they are conscious and when they are unconscious. Think of following the rule "Drive on the right-hand side of the road," for example. That rule functions causally both consciously and unconsciously. But unconscious rule-following, like conscious rule-following, must be a matter of following the intentional content of the rule, and it must operate in real time. The time of the operation of the rule and the time of the behavior governed by the rule are the same. These features are typically not preserved in those cognitive science explanations that postulate unconscious rule-following, of rules that could not become conscious even in principle.

Naturalizing Intentionality: Another Clash of Default Positions

Our overall aim in this book is to show how various puzzling phenomena, matters of mind, language, and society, can all be shown to be part of the natural world, continuous with planets, atoms, and digestion. In the case of intentionality, this problem is supposed to be exceptionally difficult because it is hard to see how "aboutness" could be a physical feature of the world in any sense. Jerry Fodor, for example, expresses a common sort of puzzlement when he writes, "If aboutness is real it must really be something else."[1] The urge to show that intentionality is really "something else" is part of the eliminative, reductionist urge that infects much of our intellectual life. The aim is not so much to explain phenomena as to get rid of them by reducing them to less puzzling sorts of things. Thus, for example, we reduce colors to light reflectances and thereby show that red is "nothing but" a photon emission in the general range of six hundred nanometers.

To understand the urge to reduce intentionality to something more basic, consider the following puzzle. Suppose I now believe, as I do, that Clinton is president of the United States. Whatever else that belief might be, it is a state of my brain. Now here is the puzzle. How can that state of my brain—consisting in such things as configurations of neurons and synaptic connections, activated by neurotransmitters—*stand for* anything? How can a state of my brain reach all the way to Washington, D.C., and pick out one man among millions? Indeed, how can any state of my brain stand for, be about, or represent anything? Are we supposed to think I send out intentional rays several thousand miles, all the way to D.C.? How tiring that must be! And why isn't it even more tiring to think the sun is shining and thus send out my intentional rays ninety-three million miles to the sun? Notice that it is no use saying that it is just like words standing for things, that my belief about Clinton stands for Clinton in just the way the word *Clinton* stands for Clinton, because that would only push the mystery back a step. How can the word stand for Clinton or anything else? The answer can only be that the word stands for Clinton because we intentionally use it to stand for Clinton. But now we are left with the problem we started with. How can I, just by uttering a word or making a mark on paper, *refer* to something far away or indeed refer to anything at all? The noise I produce is just a noise like any other, and the marks on paper are just marks. What remarkable feat do I perform to give them these amazing capacities? The problem, in short, is that we cannot explain the intentionality of the mind by appealing to the intentionality of language, because the intentionality of language already depends on the intentionality of the mind. If we are to think that the belief in my brain has intentionality because I use it in the way I use the sentences that come out of my mouth, we are left with a homunculus fallacy. I have to suppose there is a little person inside my head who is imposing intentionality on the belief in the way that I impose intentionality on the sentence.

I believe that most of what philosophers have said by way of attempting to solve this problem is woefully inadequate. Daniel Dennett tells us that the homunculus fallacy is not really a fallacy because we can replace an intelligent homunculus with a whole army of progressively stupider homunculi.[2] Fodor tells us that intentionality is just a matter of objects in the world causing "tokenings" of words and other symbols in our heads.[3] I am not going to criticize these answers in detail here because I want to spend the time developing a totally different sort of account. So, briefly: Dennett's answer won't do because it still leaves us with a homunculus fallacy. The "progressively stupider" homunculi still have to have intentionality if they are going to perform their homuncular tasks. Fodor's answer won't do because nonintentional causal relations will always be insufficient to account for intentionality. You can always get the causal relations without the intentionality. Suppose the sight of cows and only cows makes me sneeze. All the same, my "tokenings" of cow effects in the form of sneezes have no intentionality; they are just sneezes. They do not stand for cows because they do not stand for anything. Suppose that sometimes a horse causes me to sneeze because it looks like a cow. So my tokenings of horse effects in the form of sneezing are counterfactually dependent on my tokenings of cow effects: horses would not make me sneeze if cows did not. This example meets all of Fodor's conditions for intentionality but there is no intentionality.

What then is the right way to "naturalize" intentionality? The first step is to see that the way we have been posing the question is altogether the wrong way to see the matter. We take an isolated intentional state—my belief that Clinton is president—we identify it with a state of my brain, and we then ask: How can that brain state have these remarkable properties? This is typical of philosophical puzzles: to solve the puzzle we have to look at the matter without making the usual presuppositions we have been making in the past.

What we find in discussions of intentionality, in short, is the same sort of clash of default positions that we find in discussions of the mind-body problem. The clash is more subtle, but it is there. One default position is that it is just a plain fact about us that we have intrinsic intentional states. Our beliefs, for example, are about objects and states of affairs in the world. The other default position, however, is that in a world consisting entirely of physical entities, it is impossible that one physical entity should be *simply about* another. The standard way in contemporary philosophy to try to resolve this clash is to find some *other* relation between physical objects and to reduce intentionality to that relation. The favorite relation nowadays is causation: one object can be about another because it stands in certain causal relations to it.

This is typical of philosophical problems that seem insoluble. We are presented with two alternatives, neither of which seems acceptable by itself but neither of which does it seem possible to abandon. But, we are told, we must choose. The history of the subject then becomes a battle between the two sides. In the case of consciousness and the mind-body problem, we were told that we had to choose between dualism, which insists on the irreducibility of the mental, and materialism, which insists that consciousness must be reducible and hence eliminable in favor of some purely physical or material account of the mind. The way we solve the problem in the case of mind-body relations—and this is typical of solutions to clashing default positions in philosophy—is to go behind the problem to examine the assumptions that both sides are making. The lesson that we learned in our investigation of the mind-body problem was not to accept these assumptions of the disputants without question.

Before applying these lessons to the study of intentionality we need to make a crucial distinction. Failure to make this obvious distinction is responsible for much of the philosophical confusion in theories of intentionality. We need to distinguish the intentionality that humans and animals have intrinsically from the sort of derived intentionality of words and sentences, pictures, diagrams, and graphs. Furthermore, we need to distinguish both of these from metaphorical attributions of intentionality, which do not literally make any claims of intentionality but are purely "as-if." Consider the claims made in statements of these three sorts.

1. I am very hungry right now.
2. In French, "J'ai grand faim en ce moment" means I am very hungry right now.
3. The plants in my garden are hungry for nutrients.

All three of these statements make reference to the intentional phenomenon of hunger, but the status of the three attributions is quite different. The first attributes intrinsic intentionality to me. If I have the state that is attributed to me, I have it regardless of what anyone else thinks about it. The second statement also literally attributes intentionality, but the intentionality of the French sentence is not intrinsic; rather, it is derived from the intrinsic intentionality of French speakers. That very sentence might have been used by the French to mean something else, or it might have meant nothing at all, and in that sense its meaning is not intrinsic to the sentence but is derived from agents who have intrinsic intentionality. All linguistic meaning is derived intentionality. (More about this in chapter 6.)

The third statement does not literally attribute any intentionality at all. The "hunger" my garden plants manifest is purely as-if. They are wilting for lack of nutrients, and I describe their condition on analogy with people and animals. I ascribe to them an intentionality they do not in fact have, though they behave as if they had intentionality. So there are two kinds of genuine intentionality, intrinsic and derived, but as-if intentionality is not a third kind. Ascriptions of as-if intentionality are metaphorical. To say that an entity has as-if intentionality is just a way of saying that it behaves as if it had intentionality, when it does not.

The distinction between intrinsic and derived intentionality is a special case of a much more fundamental distinction between those features of the world that are *observer-independent*, such as force, mass, and gravitational attraction, and those features that are *observer-dependent*, such as being a knife, or a chair, or a sentence of English. Intrinsic intentionality is observer-independent—I have my state of hunger regardless of what any observer thinks. Derived intentionality is observer-dependent—it is only in relation to observers, users, and so on, that, for example, a sentence of French has the meaning it has.

These distinctions are important for other issues we will discuss later on, but at present our target is intrinsic intentionality. All derived intentionality is derived from the intrinsic. It is important to emphasize this because in the present era many authors have treated derived and as-if intentionality as paradigmatic and tried to explain all intrinsic intentionality in terms of them. Thus, the derived intentionality of computer operations is treated as the model for studying the intrinsic intentionality in the human brain, and the as-if ascriptions are sometimes even treated as the correct model for understanding the sorts of ascriptions we are making to humans when we attribute intrinsic intentionality to them.[4] The basic thesis I am advancing, a thesis that differs from what is currently standard and orthodox in cognitive science, can be put as follows. Suppose we had a complete science of physics, chemistry, and biology. Then at the end of the day certain features would be established as real, observer-independent, or intrinsic features of the real world. In physics these would include, for example, gravitation and electromagnetism. In biology they would include, for example, mitosis, meiosis, and photosynthesis. My claim is that they would also include consciousness and intentionality. Consciousness and intentionality, though features of the mind, are observer-independent in the sense that if I am conscious or have an intentional state such as thirst, those features do not depend for their existence on what anyone outside me thinks. They are not, like sentences of a language, only the things they are because outsiders think that is what they are. In earlier chapters, we naturalized consciousness by showing how it can be a natural biological phenomenon. My task now is to naturalize intentionality by showing how the intrinsic intentionality of humans and other animals can be part of the natural world.

Intentionality Naturalized as a Biological Phenomenon

So here goes. Let's start with simple cases. The most biologically primitive forms of intentionality are those forms of desire that involve bodily needs such as hunger and thirst. Both of these are intentional because both are forms of desire. Hunger is a desire to eat, thirst is a desire to drink. Here is how thirst works. A lack of water in the system causes the kidneys to secrete renin, and the renin acts on a circulating peptide, called "angiotensin," to make angiotensin 2. This substance gets into the brain and attacks portions of the hypothalamus, causing an increase in the rate of neuron-firing in those portions. This in turn causes the animal to feel a conscious desire to drink.

Now, please do not say that it could not cause any such thing because it would be crossing the mind-body chasm, the explanatory gap between mental and physical. We know that such neurobiological processes just do, as a matter of brute biological fact, cause such conscious intentional states as thirst and hunger. That is how nature works. Additional evidence for the role of the hypothalamus in the causation of certain sorts of thirst is provided by the fact that patients with certain sorts of tumors pressing on the hypothalumus feel thirsty all the time. No amount of drinking can assuage their thirst. And patients with lesions in the relevant portions of the hypothalamus never feel thirsty.

Notice also that there is a tremendous evolutionary advantage to having these sorts of conscious intentional phenomena.

Just as there is an evolutionary advantage to conscious feeling of pain—because the animal tries to resist and avoid the injuries to its body that cause pain, and treats existing injuries to lessen pain—so the conscious feelings of thirst lead the animal to consume the water on which its survival depends.

A word of qualification: the actual account I give is a standard neurobiology textbook account, and no doubt as we come to know more it will seem wonderfully quaint, outdated, and oversimplified. Certainly the hypothalamic events by themselves are unlikely to be sufficient for any conscious states. There have to be all sorts of connections with other parts of the brain. But the point of the example is to explain how an account like this one *could* give a neurological, and therefore a naturalistic, explanation of a certain form of intentionality.

Once you grant me such a biological explanation of any form of intentionality, then I have an entering wedge for undermining the whole set of assumptions that made the alternatives seem the only ones available. Once we see how thirst can be a form of natural biological intentionality, then it is not too hard to extend the same sort of explanation to the sensory modalities, such as vision and touch. Indeed, for the case of vision in chapter 1, I gave a sketch of how the impact of photons on the retina eventually causes a visual experience in the brain. Any standard textbook of neurobiology contains a chapter on vision explaining how the stimulus of the peripheral nerve endings eventually causes a visual experience. I do not wish to suggest, of course, that we now have the final answer to how brain processes cause visual experiences. We do not know the answer to that question, and we are not likely to find the answer in the near future. The point I am making is simply that we know the *form* of the answer. We know that we are looking for causal mechanisms in the brain.

Now, and this is the point, once we reach the actual visual experience, we have the intrinsic intentionality we have been looking for. There is no way I could have *this* visual experience I am actually having without it at least seeming to me that there is a computer screen in front of me.

But, the skeptic will ask, what fact about the visual experience makes that very experience one of seeming to see a computer screen? Notice what an odd question that is. I believe the only answer it can have is: it is internal to this very experience, as a conscious event in the world, that it has exactly this intentionality. It is part of the visual experience that, in having it, it seems to me that I am seeing a computer screen in front of me. Thus, the urge to naturalize intentionality and the feeling that the only form of naturalization is some form of reduction is a double mistake. First, there is the mistake of wondering how mere matter can refer, but underlying that is the deeper mistake of wondering how *anything* can refer. And the hidden agenda behind the second mistake is the suggestion that maybe *nothing* can refer intrinsically. The way we remove the first mistake is an extension of our solution to the mind-body problem: we simply go behind the question to look at its presuppositions. We find the presupposition that either intentionality is mysterious and inexplicable, on the one hand, or it really is something else, that it is eliminable by an eliminative reduction, on the other. The answer to this mistake, like the answer to the mind-body problem, is to reject both alternatives.

But the answer to the second mistake requires us to go beyond our solution to the mind-body problem and look at some special features of intrinsic intentionality. If we try to treat, for example, our conscious visual experiences as if they were just phenomena in the world like stones or trees or digestion, then it seems a miracle that they could refer. But of course, though they are natural processes, they have a special feature. It is internal to the state that it has this intentionality. It could not be this very visual experience if it was not an experience whose intentionality was that it is a case of seeming to see this thing in front of me.

But why is that part not obvious? Why would anyone ignore or wish to deny that? Two reasons. The first is the failure to distinguish intrinsic, derived, and as-if intentionality. If you start with derived intentionality of the sort we get in words and sentences, or even worse, if you start with as-if intentionality of the sort you get in metaphorical ascriptions of intentionality, then reference or aboutness is going to seem mysterious. Surely, it seems, there has to be a homunculus somewhere to impose intentionality on the phenomena. A second source of the mistake is to neglect the centrality of consciousness. If you think intentionality has no essential connection to consciousness, then it will seem to you that there are all kinds of intentionality in the world, and you will try to analyze it in terms of causal relations or some such. The way out is to start with intrinsic intentionality in its conscious forms. There can indeed be an interesting question: How does this word *Clinton* come to stand for Clinton? The word, after all, has only derived intentionality. Then there are interesting questions concerning the nature of the derivation and the form of the intentionality, once derived. But there can't be an interesting question of the sort: How can this conscious visual experience be a case of seeming to see something? That is, once we have the visual experience with all its features, and once we have given neurobiological and psychological explanations of those features, there cannot be a further interesting philosophical question as to how it can be a case of seeming to see something, because the seeming to see is not *added on* to the visual experience in a way that the referential relation to a particular man is added on to the word *Clinton*. The experience just is an experience of seeming to see something.

Our earlier insistence on the distinctions between intrinsic intentionality, on the one hand, and derived and as-if, on the other, and our equal insistence on the primacy of consciousness were not innocent. They are what enable us to overcome the conflict of the two default positions.

The Structure of Intentional States

I have so far been talking about intentionality in somewhat vague terms. Intentionality, as I have defined it, is simply that feature of mental states by which they are directed at or about objects and states of affairs other than themselves. Just as an arrow can be fired at a target and miss, or fired even if there is no target there, so an intentional state can be directed at an object and be misdirected, or fail altogether because there is no object there. A child can believe that that man is Santa Claus when in fact he is a department store employee, and one can believe that ghosts are present in this house even if there are no such things as ghosts. But what a peculiar relation, then, intentionality must be, if intentionality can be directed at what does not even exist. How is such a thing possible?

The Distinction Between the Type and the Content of Intentional States

To understand the structure of intentional states, we need to make some basic distinctions at the outset of our investigation. First of all, for any intentional state—belief, desire, hope, fear, visual perception, or intention to perform an action—we need to make a distinction between the content of the state and the type of state that it is. Thus, for example, you can hope that it will rain, fear that it will rain, and believe that it will rain. In each case, we have the same content—that it will rain—but that content is presented in different intentional modes. This distinction between content and mode carries over to perceptions and intentional actions. You can see that it is raining, just as you can believe that it is raining, and you can intend to go to the movies, just as you can wish that you were going to the movies. In all these examples, the contents are entire propositions and thus have truth conditions, or as I prefer to say, "conditions of satisfaction."

We need a notion more general than the notion of truth because we need a notion that covers not only those intentional states like beliefs that can be true or false, but states like desires and intentions, which can be fulfilled or frustrated, carried out or not carried out. Just as I can believe that I will go to the movies tonight, and thus have a state that is true or false, so I can desire to go to the movies tonight or intend to go to the movies tonight. But my desires and intentions cannot be literally true or false. What stands to my belief as its truth condition—that I go to the movies tonight—is exactly what stands to my desire as its fulfillment condition—that I go to the movies tonight. I will say then that such intentional states as beliefs and desires have *conditions of satisfaction*, a term that covers truth conditions for belief, fulfillment conditions for desires, carrying-out conditions for intentions, and so on. Having conditions of satisfaction is a general feature of a very large number of intentional states with a propositional content, and truth conditions are a special case of conditions of satisfaction.

This distinction between truth conditions and other kinds of conditions of satisfaction leads to the next structural feature of intentional states.

Direction of Fit

It is a remarkable feature of the mind that it relates us by way of intentionality to the real world. That is what intentionality is—the special way the mind has of relating us to the world. Equally remarkable is the fact that there are different ways in which intentional contents are related to the world by different types of intentional states. The different types of intentional states relate the propositional content to the real world with, so to speak, different obligations of fitting. Beliefs and hypotheses are said to be true or false depending on whether the world really is the way the belief represents it as being. For this reason, I say that beliefs have the mind-to-world direction of fit. It is the responsibility, so to speak, of the belief to match an independently existing world. Desires and intentions, on the other hand, do not have the mind-to-world direction of fit, because if a desire or intention is not satisfied, it is the responsibility, so to speak, not of the desire or intention, but of the world, that it fails to match the content of the desire or intention. The terminology of "direction of fit" was invented by J. L. Austin,[5] but the best example to illustrate the distinction was given by G. E. M. Anscombe.[6] In Anscombe's type of example, a woman gives her husband a shopping list on which are written the words: *beer*, *butter*, and *bacon*. The man takes the list to the supermarket and puts things in the cart to match the items on the list. The list functions like an order or a desire and thus has the world-to-list direction of fit. It is the responsibility of the man to try to make the world match the contents of the list. He tries to make the world, in the form of the purchases, fit or match the items on his list. But suppose the man is followed by a detective, and the detective writes down what the man puts down in the shopping cart. The detective writes *beer*, *butter*, and *bacon*, so that when they reach the checkout counter, both man and detective have identical lists. However, the function of the lists is radically different. It is the responsibility of the detective's list to match an independently existing reality. The list functions as a description or as a report of what has actually happened. His list is just supposed to be a representation of how things are. The husband's list functions to enable him to change reality to match the contents of the list. The point of the husband's list is not to describe reality, to represent how things are, but to change reality so that it matches the list. The husband's list has the world-to-list direction of fit. The detective's list has the list-to-world direction of fit. In our language, there is a special vocabulary for describing those representations that succeed or fail in achieving list(or word)-to-world direction of fit: they are said to be either "true" or "false." Truth or falsity, in short, name success or failure in achieving word-to-world direction of fit.

You can see the distinction very clearly if you imagine what happens in the case of a mistake. Suppose the detective gets home and realizes that he made a mistake. The man did not take bacon, he took pork chops. The detective can simply correct things by crossing out the word *bacon* and writing in the words *pork chop*. The list is now correct in achieving list-to-world direction of fit. But if the husband gets home and his wife says, "You idiot, I wrote *bacon* on the list, but you brought pork chops instead," the man cannot correct the situation by saying, "That's all right, honey. I'll just cross out *bacon* and write in *pork chops*." The reason for this distinction is that the husband, unlike the detective, has the responsibility of making the world fit the list. The detective has the responsibility of making the list fit the world. What is true of the relation of the lists to the world is true of words and the world, and indeed of the mind and the world. The distinction between list-to-world and world-to-list is an instance of the more general distinctions between word-to-world and world-to-word as well as mind-to-world and world-to-mind directions of fit. I hope this distinction is clear. I believe it is crucial for any theory of intentionality. Beliefs, perceptions, and memories have the mind-to-world direction of fit, because their aim is to represent how things are; desires and intentions have the world-to-mind direction of fit because their aim is to represent not how things are but how we would like them to be or how we plan to make them be.

So far, we have two features in our general account of the structure of intentional states—the distinction between propositional content and type of intentional state, and the notion of direction of fit, together with the idea of different directions of fit. We can now introduce some complexities to each of these two features. The first complexity to point out is that not all intentional states have entire propositions as their contents. Thus, if a man is in love with Mary or hates Bill, then the content of these intentional states refers to Mary or Bill, and the attitude he has is either love or hate. Another complexity derives from the fact that not all intentional states have the world-to-mind or the mind-to-world direction of fit. Some, indeed, presuppose that the fitting has already taken place. For example, if you are sorry that you have insulted a friend or you are glad that the sun is shining, in each case you have an intentional state in which it is presupposed that the propositional content is already satisfied, that you have insulted your friend and that the sun is shining. For such cases, I say that they have the *null direction of fit*. In the way that the aim of beliefs is to be true and thus achieve the mind-to-world direction of fit, and the aim of desires is to be fulfilled and thus achieve the world-to-mind direction of fit, being glad or sorry does not have that kind of aim, even though each intentional state has propositional contents that may or may not be satisfied. To account for this distinction, I just say the direction of fit is null.

Conditions of Satisfaction

We can now unify these various points about intentionality by describing the feature that constitutes them as intentional. I already alluded to this feature briefly when I introduced the notion of conditions of satisfaction. I believe that the key to understanding intentionality is conditions of satisfaction. An intentional state is satisfied if the world is the way it is represented by the intentional state as being. Beliefs can be true or false, desires can be fulfilled or frustrated, intentions can be carried out or not carried out. In each case, the intentional state is satisfied or not depending on whether there is indeed a match between propositional content and the reality represented.

It is a general feature of intentional states with a propositional content that they have conditions of satisfaction. Indeed, if one wanted a slogan for analyzing intentionality, I believe it should be this: "By their conditions of satisfaction shall ye know them." If we want to know exactly what a person's intentional state is, we must ask ourselves under what conditions exactly would it be satisfied or not satisfied. Those intentional states that do not have an entire propositional content, such as love and hate, and thus do not have conditions of satisfaction are, I believe, partly constituted by intentional states that do have an entire propositional content and thus do have conditions of satisfaction. So, one cannot love a person, for example, without having a set of beliefs and desires regarding that person. And those beliefs and desires are, in large part, constitutive of the love that one has for that person. Thus, though superficially love does not have conditions of satisfaction, any actual case of one human loving another is constituted in large part by a set of intentional states that do have conditions of satisfaction. Those intentional states that have an entire propositional content, such as shame and pride, but no direction of fit are in large part constituted by beliefs and desires, which do have a direction of fit; thus, the intentional states with no direction of fit do have conditions of satisfaction. For example, if I am proud that I won the race, then I must at least (a) believe that I won the race and (b) find it desirable or want it to be the case that I won the race.

Intentional Causation

I have said that intentionality is that feature of the mind whereby it intrinsically represents objects and states of affairs in the world. But our minds are also in constant causal contact with the world. When we see things, the objects we see cause our visual experiences of them. When we remember events in our past, those past events cause our present memories. When we intend to move our bodies, those intentions cause the bodily movements. In each case, we find both a causal and an intentional component. It is essential to the functioning of intentionality, and indeed essential to our survival in the world, that the representing capacity of the mind and the causal relations to the world should mesh in some systematic way. The form in which they do is *intentional causation*. This form of causation differs dramatically from billiard ball or Humean causation: the cause and effect work in the way they do because either the cause is a representation of the effect or the effect is a representation of the cause. Here are some examples of how it works. If I want to drink water, and I then drink water by way of satisfying my desire to drink water, then my mental state, the desire (that I drink water), causes it to be the case that I drink water. The desire in this case both causes and represents its condition of satisfaction. Sometimes it is part of the conditions of satisfaction of the intentional state itself that it is only satisfied if it functions causally. Thus, for example, if I intend to raise my arm, then the intention requires more to be satisfied than just that I raise my arm. Rather, it is part of the conditions of satisfaction of my intention to raise my arm that that very intention should cause the raising of my arm. For this reason, I say that intentions are causally self-referential.[7] The intention is satisfied only if the intention itself causes the rest of its conditions of satisfaction. I will succeed in carrying out my intention to raise my arm only if (a) I do raise my arm and (b) my intention to raise my arm causes my raising of my arm.

Such causal self-referentiality is present not only in the "volitive" states, such as intentions, but also in the "cognitive" states of perception and memory. Thus, for example, if I really see that tree, then it must not only be the case that I have a visual experience whose conditions of satisfaction are that there is a tree there, but the fact that there is a tree there must cause the very visual experience that has those conditions of satisfaction. Similarly with memory. If I remember running a ski race in Val d'Isère, then it is part of the conditions of satisfaction of the memory not only that I really did run such a ski race, but the event of my running the race must cause the memory that has those conditions of satisfaction. In the case of cognitive states with causal self-referentiality, such as perception and memory, we have mind-to-world direction of fit and world-to-mind direction of causation. My mental state of memory or perception "fits" the world only if the world causes the state that has the fit. In volitive states, such as intentions, the directions are reversed. My intention to raise my arm "fits" the world only if the state itself causes the event in the world that it fits, that is, only if the intention itself causes the event of my raising my arm.

Intentional causation is absolutely crucial in understanding the explanation of human behavior and thus in understanding the differences between the natural sciences and the social sciences. Human behavior, where rational, functions on the basis of reasons, but the reasons explain the behavior only if the relation between the reason and the behavior is both logical and causal. Explanations of rational human behavior thus essentially employ the apparatus of intentional causation. For example, suppose we explain Hitler's invasion of Russia by saying he wanted Lebensraum in the East. That explanation makes sense to us because we suppose that (a) Hitler wanted Lebensraum in the East, (b) he believed he could get Lebensraum by invading Russia, and (c) a and b together, by intentional causation, provide at least part of the causal explanation of the decision, hence the intention, to invade Russia, and (d) the intention to invade Russia is at least part of the cause of the invasion of Russia, by intentional causation.

It is important to emphasize that such explanations are not deterministic in form. The form of an intentionalistic explanation of behavior does not imply that the action had to occur, that the intentional causes are sufficient to determine that the action had to be performed. Nor are they deterministic in practice except in odd pathological cases. When I explain my own behavior by stating the beliefs and desires that motivated me to act, I do not normally imply that I could not have done otherwise. Typically when I reason from my desires and beliefs as to what I should do, there is a *gap* between the causes of my decision in the form of beliefs and desires and the actual decision, and there is another gap between the decision and the performance of the action. The reason for these gaps is that the intentionalistic causes of behavior are not sufficient to determine the behavior. Some exceptions to this are cases of addiction, obsession, overwhelming passion, and other forms of pathology. When I decide whom to vote for in an election, the intentionalistic explanation of my behavior does not give causally sufficient conditions. This contrasts with the heroin addict taking a drug because he wants heroin and believes the drug is heroin. In this case, the addict cannot help himself, and the explanation does give causally sufficient conditions. The name usually given to this gap is "the freedom of the will." It remains an unsolved problem in philosophy how there can be freedom of the will, given that there are no corresponding gaps in the brain.

The Background of Intentionality

Intentional states do not function in isolation. In order that I can believe that Clinton is the president of the United States, or intend to go skiing next weekend, or hope that my income tax will be lower this year than it was last year, I also have to have a lot of other intentional states. For example, to have these states I have to have the belief that the United States is a republic, the belief that there are ski areas within reachable distance of my house, and the belief that the United States has a system of income tax for its citizens. However, in addition to all these beliefs as well as other intentional states, I have to have a set of capacities and presuppositions that enable me to cope with the world. It is this set of capacities, abilities, ten-

dencies, habits, dispositions, taken-for-granted presuppositions, and "know-how" generally that I have been calling the
"Background," and the general thesis of the Background that I
have been presupposing throughout this book is that all of our
intentional states, all of our particular beliefs, hopes, fears, and
so on, only function in the way they do—that is, they only determine their conditions of satisfaction—against a Background
of know-how that enables me to cope with the world.

The best way to see this point, I believe, is to take any example of a real-life intentional state and see what other
things I have to presuppose in order that the intentional state
can function. Right now I have the intention to go to a bookstore to buy some books and to a restaurant to eat lunch.
This complex intention presupposes an enormous metaphysical apparatus. Some of that apparatus is on the surface in the
form of beliefs and desires. For example, I desire only certain
sorts of books, and I believe a particular restaurant is the
best in the neighborhood. But underneath these conscious
thoughts is a vast apparatus that is in a sense too fundamental
to be thought of as just more beliefs and desires. For example, I know how to walk and how to behave in bookstores
and restaurants; I take it for granted that the floor underneath me will support me and that my body will move as a
single unified entity without flying apart; I take it for granted
that the books in the bookstore will be readable though not
edible, and the food in the restaurant edible though not readable. Knowing how to deal with these situations, I have the
ability to eat by putting food in my mouth but not in my ear
and the ability to read by holding books in front of my eyes
but not by rubbing them against my stomach. One can imagine a science fiction world in which it is all different, in which
one eats by scanning with one's eyes and reads by chewing
and swallowing, but I do not hold a *hypothesis* to the effect
that I live in this sort of world and not that sort of world.
Rather, I just take a huge metaphysics for granted.

Part of the Background is common to all cultures. For example, we all walk upright and eat by putting food in our mouths. Such universal phenomena I call the "deep Background," but many other Background presuppositions vary from culture to culture. For example, in my culture we eat pigs and cows but not worms and grasshoppers, and we eat at certain times of day and not others. On such matters cultures vary, and I call such features of the Background "local cultural practices." There is of course no sharp dividing line between deep Background and local cultural practices.

The point I wish to emphasize for our present investigation is that intentionality does not function as a separate mental capacity. Intentional states function the way they do only given a presupposed set of Background capacities that are not just more intentional states. The Background is, in an important sense, pre-intentional. In order that my intention to buy books and eat lunch can determine what I am to do—that is, determine its conditions of satisfaction—I have to have a lot of capacities that are not part of that intention and not part of the set of my other intentional states. Thinking of intentionality in this way, as a set of thought processes that work the way they do only against a Background of unthought capacities, opens up a number of fields of investigation that go beyond the scope of this book but still deserve mention. For example, we usually think of rationality as a matter of intentionally following rules of rationality. I think rather that our capacity for rational thought and behavior is for the most part a Background capacity. Furthermore, we usually think of neurosis as a matter of irrational and often repressed beliefs and desires. Much neurosis is of this type, but some is Background neurosis. For example, the patient is too rigid in his dealings with himself and other people. It is not just that he has irrational beliefs and desires, but he has a stance toward his experiences that makes it impossible for him to cope in a flexible, accommodating, and creative way.

FIVE

The Structure of the Social Universe: How the Mind Creates an Objective Social Reality

My aim in this book is to explain the general structure of several of the philosophically most puzzling parts of reality—mind, language, and society—and then explain how they fit together. In so doing, I am taking a lot for granted. We know a lot more about how the world works than our grandparents did, and we can rely on that knowledge—a knowledge derived from physics, chemistry, biology, and the other special sciences. Standing on the great achievements of the past, we can get a better view. In this book, I have simply been taking the results of physics, chemistry, biology, and especially neurobiology for granted. I have so far tried to give an account of the mind that is consistent with the fact that the mind is essentially a biological phenomenon and that therefore its two most important interrelated features, consciousness and intentionality, are also biological. In this chapter, I use my account of the mind to explain the nature of social and institutional reality. Let's begin by stating the philosophical problem.

Social and Institutional Reality

Think, for example, about the piece of paper that I have in my wallet. If I take it out of my wallet to inspect it, I see that its physical properties are rather uninteresting. It consists, chemically speaking, of cellulose fibers stained with certain dyes. However, in spite of its trivial physics and chemistry, all of us regard it as of some importance. The reason for this is that it is money. If we ask, "What facts about it make it money?" we find that the chemistry and the physics are insufficient to answer the question. If I try to produce something that looks exactly like this piece of paper, even if I duplicate it exactly down to the last molecule, it would not be money. On the contrary, it would be counterfeit, and I would be subject to arrest and prosecution. So, once again, what facts about it make it money? The beginnings of an answer can be given by saying that a type of phenomenon is money only if we think it is money. Being thought to be money is a necessary but not a sufficient condition. For something to be money there has to be more than just a set of attitudes, even though the attitudes are partly constitutive, and essentially constitutive, of a type of phenomenon being money. I have to say "type" because particular token instances might be counterfeit. A particular bill might be thought to be money, when in fact it is counterfeit. The general point remains: a type of thing is money over the long haul only if it is accepted as money. And what goes for money, goes for social and institutional reality generally. So, money, language, property, marriage, government, universities, cocktail parties, lawyers, presidents of the United States are all partly—but not entirely—constituted under these descriptions by the fact that we regard them as such. An object fits one of these descriptions in part because we think that it does, or we accept or recognize it as such. Furthermore, important consequences follow from the fact that we regard these phenomena as fitting a certain description: from the fact that I and others think that the piece of paper in my pocket is money, I have certain powers that I would not otherwise have. And what is true of money is true of institutional reality generally. From the facts that I am a citizen, or a convicted criminal, or the host at a cocktail party, or the owner of a car, certain powers—including negative powers such as responsibilities and penalties and positive powers such as rights and entitlements—accrue to me. These phenomena ought to puzzle us as philosophers, and the question I want to address in this chapter is: How do such social and institutional phenomena fit into the overall ontology described in the preceding chapters? What is the ontology of the social and the institutional? How can there be an objective reality that is what it is only because we think it is what it is? When I go into a store and present these bits of paper to the clerk, he does not say, "Well, perhaps *you* think it is money, but why should we care what you think?"

Our main problem in this chapter is to explain how there can be an epistemically objective social reality that is partly constituted by an ontologically subjective set of attitudes. Just to nail the problem down a little more specifically, there are several puzzling features that follow from this combination of the subjective and the objective that we would like to be able to explain. I will mention three of these.

First, there is a peculiar form of circularity in the account that I have given so far, and we need to make sure that this circularity is not vicious, that it is not destructive of any possible analysis. The circularity is this: If something is only money or property or marriage because it is believed to be money or property or marriage, then, we have to ask, what exactly is the content of the belief in each case? If we must believe that the piece of paper in my pocket is money if it is to be money, then it looks as if the content of the belief that it is money can't be just that it is money, for its being money requires that it be believed to be money. And if so, the content of the belief has to be in part that it is believed to be believed to be money. But we would then have to ask the question all over again, and the answer, once again, would be: part of the content of the belief is that it is believed to be believed to be believed to be money. This necessity of repeating the question generates either circularity or an infinite regress in the definition of money, and it seems we would never be able to state what the content of the belief is when something is believed to be money. And thus we would never be able to explain money without circularity or infinite regress. To avoid this regress we need to explain the concept of money as it occurs in the belief that something is money, without using the concept of money.

A second puzzling feature derives from the few remarks that I have already made. How can institutional reality function causally? If money is only money because it is believed to be money, and similarly for the other examples that I gave, then how is it that money can act causally? How does it come about that in a world consisting entirely of physical and chemical elements there is a causal efficacy to the institutional reality of money, governments, universities, private property, marriages, and so on? As will have been clear from earlier chapters, in philosophical studies we have to begin by approaching the problems naively. We have to allow ourselves to be astounded by facts that any sane person would take for granted. The astounding fact we are facing now is that the institutional reality of property, money, marriage, and government functions causally in our lives. But how could it? Institutions don't have force, mass, or gravitational attraction. What is the equivalent of the law F = MA where institutional reality is concerned?

A third feature that relates to the other two is this: What exactly is the role of language in institutional reality? I said that something is money, property, or marriage only if people think it is money, property, or marriage, but how could they even have such a thought if they did not have a language? Moreover, is not language precisely the sort of institutional reality that we are trying to explain? One way to state this third puzzle is to note that in institutional reality, language is not used merely to *describe* the facts but, in an odd way, is partly *constitutive* of the facts. When, for example, it says on a twenty-dollar bill, "This note is legal tender for all debts public and private," the U.S. Treasury is not *describing* a fact but in part *creating* one. The utterance is like a performative, even though it lacks a performative verb. Performative utterances are those in which saying something makes it true. The main verb in the sentence, the performative verb, names the act performed in the utterance of the sentence. For example, if I say, in the appropriate circumstance, "I promise to come and see you," or, "I resign," saying these things is promising or resigning. In these cases, I create the fact that the utterance is a promise or a resignation just by saying it is. Performative utterances are very common in the creation of institutional facts. The creation of legal tender by the Treasury when it states that the currency it issues is legal tender is like a performative in that it creates the fact it describes. Indeed, one aspect of this third puzzle that we need to explain is the role of performative utterances in the creation of institutional facts.

I have stated these puzzles rather generally, and even naively, because I want you to get a feel for them before we begin to develop the apparatus necessary for the solution.

Observer-Dependency and the Building Blocks of Social Reality

It seems to me that in order to account for social and institutional reality we need to clarify one fundamental distinction and introduce three new elements into the explanatory apparatus we have been using so far. The distinction is the one that I introduced in chapter 4 between those features of the world that exist independently of our attitudes and intentionality generally and those features that exist only relative to our intentionality. I call this the distinction between observer-dependent and observer-independent features of the world. The three elements are collective intentionality, the assignment of function, and a certain form of rules that I call "constitutive rules."

The Distinction Between Observer-Independent and Observer-Dependent

Some of the features of the world exist entirely independently of us humans and of our attitudes and activities; others depend on us. Consider, for example, an object that has both of these sorts of features, the thing I am now sitting on. This object has a certain mass and a certain molecular configuration, and these exist independently of us. Mass and molecular structure are observer-independent features of the world. But this object also has the feature that it is a chair. The fact that it is a chair is a result of its having been designed, manufactured, sold, bought, and used as a chair. Such features as being a chair are observer-relative or observer-dependent, where "observer" is short for "maker, user, designer, and intentionality possessor generally." Such features as mass, force, gravitational attraction, and voltage level are observer-independent; such features as being money, property, a knife, a chair, a football game, or a nice day for a picnic are observer-dependent or observer-relative. In general, the natural sciences deal with features that are observer-independent, such as force, mass, and photosynthesis; the social sciences deal with features that are observer-relative, such as elections, balance-of-payments problems, and social organizations.

Notice that the intentionality that creates observer-relative phenomena is not itself observer-relative. The fact that this object is a chair depends on, among other things, our attitudes, but those attitudes are not themselves observer-relative. When we create observer-relative phenomena through the exercise of our intentionality, that intentionality does not depend on any further intentionality. Once we have an attitude, it does not matter whether anyone else thinks we have that attitude.

The distinction between observer-independent and observer-relative features of reality was already prefigured in chapter 3 by our distinction between intrinsic and derived intentionality. The intrinsic intentionality exemplified by my present state of hunger, though it is ontologically subjective, is observer-independent. It does not depend on anybody's attitudes about me or it. The derived intentionality exemplified by the fact that the French sentence "J'ai faim" means "I am hungry" is observer-dependent. The sentence has that derived intentionality (that is, meaning) only because French speakers use it with that meaning.

I think the distinction between observer-relative and observer-independent features is much more important than such traditional distinctions in our philosophical culture as the distinctions between mind and body or fact and value. In a sense, this book is in part about that distinction and its consequences. In this chapter, for example, we are concerned with the fact that a set of observer-relative institutional phenomena can have an epistemically objective existence even though their ontology is observer-dependent and thus contains an element that is ontologically subjective.

Now I turn to the three elements that we will use in giving an account of that reality.

Collective Intentionality

In the last chapter, we discussed intentionality as if all intentionality were of the form "I intend" or "I believe" or "I hope," and so on. But there is an interesting form of intentionality that is of the form "we intend," "we believe," "we hope," and so on. Now of course, if I have a "we intention," I must also have an "I intention," because if I am intentionally doing something as part of our doing something, then I must intend to do my part. And in order to intend to do my part, I must intend that I do something that is part of our doing something. So, for example, if *we* are pushing a car in order to get it started, I have to have the intention that *I* will do my part. But all the same, it seems to me that there is an irreducible class of intentionality that is collective intentionality or "we-intentionality." How can that be? In our philosophical tradition, it has always been tempting to think of collective intentionality as reducible to individual intentionality. We think we-intentionality must always be reducible to and ultimately eliminable in favor of "I-intentionality." The reason for this temptation is that if you think that collective intentionality is irreducible, you seem to be forced to postulate some sort of collective mental entity, some overarching Hegelian World Spirit, some "we" that floats around mysteriously above us individuals and of which we as individuals are just expressions. But since all the intentionality I have is in my head and all you have is in your head, our puzzle is: How can it be the case that there is such a thing as irreducible, *collective* intentionality?

Most philosophers think that this puzzle cannot be answered in the form I just stated it, and they seek to reduce collective or we-intentionality to individual or I-intentionality. They try to reduce "we intend," "we believe," and "we hope," to "I intend," "I believe," and "I hope." They suppose that whenever two people share a collective intention, as when they are trying to do something together, then each has an intention of the "I intend" form, plus a belief about the other's intention. Thus, my intentionality, if I am part of a collective, is, "I intend to do such and such," and, "I believe that you also have that intention." Furthermore, I have to believe that you believe that I believe that you have that intention, and this then generates a nonvicious regress of the form "I believe that you believe that I believe that you believe that I believe," and so on; on your part, you believe that I believe that you believe that I believe that you believe, and so on. This sequence of iterated beliefs about beliefs on the part of two or more people is called "mutual belief."[1] Adherents of the view that collective intentionality reduces to individual intentionality, including mutual belief as a form of individual intentionality, think that the infinite regress is not vicious. We always have the potential of consciously thinking of yet a higher belief about a belief, but in practice limits of time and energy will call a halt to the upward climb of iterated beliefs.

I think this whole approach, which attempts to reduce collective intentionality to individual intentionality plus mutual belief, is confused. I don't think my head is big enough to accommodate so many beliefs, and I have a much simpler solution. Just take the collective intentionality in my head as a primitive. It is of the form "we intend" even though it is in my individual head. And if in fact I am succeeding in cooperating with you, then what is in your head will also be of the form "we intend." That will have consequences for what *I* believe and what *I* intend, because my individual intentionality derives from my collective intentionality. But in order to account for the fact that all intentionality is in the heads of individual agents, we do not have to suppose that all intentionality is of the form "I intend," "I believe," "I hope." Individual agents can have in their individual heads intentionality of the form "we intend," "we hope," and so on. To summarize this point: the requirement that all intentionality be in the heads of individual agents, a requirement that is sometimes called "methodological individualism," does not require that all intentionality be expressed in the first-person singular. There is nothing to prevent us from having in our individual heads intentionality of the form, for example, "we believe," "we intend," and so on.

I have stated all of this in very abstract and theoretical terms, but I want to remind you that in real life collective intentionality is common, practical, and indeed essential to our very existence. Look at any football game, political rally, concert performance, college classroom, church service, or conversation, and you will see collective intentionality in action. Contrast an orchestra performing a symphony with the individual members of the orchestra playing their parts in isolation. Even if by chance the individual members were all rehearsing their parts in a way that happened to be synchronized, so that it sounded like the symphony, there is still a crucial difference between the intentionality of collective cooperative behavior and that of individual behavior. What goes for the orchestra goes for a football team, the crowd at a political rally, two people dancing, and a construction crew building a house. Whenever you have people cooperating, you have collective intentionality. Whenever you have people sharing their thoughts, feelings, and so on, you have collective intentionality; and indeed, I want to say, this is the foundation of all social activities.

Even human conflict, in most of its forms, requires cooperation. Think of a prize fight, a football game, a legal trial, or even two philosophers engaged in an argument. For these sorts of conflicts to go on, there has to be a higher level of cooperation. If one man comes up behind another in a dark alley and hits him on the head, no collective intentionality is required. But for a prize fight, a wrestling match, a duel, or even an exchange of insults at a cocktail party, a level of cooperation is required. In order to be fighting at one level we have to be cooperating in having a fight at another level.

I am going to define arbitrarily a *social fact* as any fact involving two or more agents who have collective intentionality. So, for example, animals hunting together, birds cooperating in building a nest, and presumably the so-called social insects, such as ants and bees, manifest collective intentionality and thus have social facts.

Human beings have a remarkable ability that enables them to get beyond mere social facts to *institutional facts.* Humans engage in more than just sheer physical cooperation; they also talk together, own property, get married, form governments, and so on. In this chapter, I explain these institutional phenomena that extend beyond social facts.

The Assignment of Function

The second building block needed to construct institutional reality, besides collective intentionality, is the assignment of function. It is a remarkable fact about human beings and some higher animals that they are capable of using certain objects as tools. This is an instance of the more general capacity to assign functions to objects, where the function is not intrinsic to the object but has to be assigned by some outside agent or agents. Think of a monkey using a stick to reach a banana. Think of primitive peoples using a log as a bench, or using a stone for digging. All of these are cases of agents assigning a function to, or imposing a function on, some natural object. The agents exploit the natural features of the object to achieve their purposes.

At this point, having remarked on the very existence of assigned functions, I want to advance a strong thesis about the notion of functions: all functions are observer-relative in the sense I just explained. They only exist relative to observers or agents who assign the function. This fact is disguised from us by the fact that often we have discovered functions in nature. We discovered, for example, that the function of the heart is to pump blood. But remember, we could only make that discovery within the context of a presupposed teleology. It is only because we take it for granted that life and survival are to be valued that we can say the *function* of the heart is to pump blood, meaning that, in the overall ecology of the organism, pumping blood serves the purposes of life and survival.

Think, for example, of the difference between saying that, just as a matter of fact, the heart causes the pumping of blood and the pumping of blood has a whole lot of other causal relations, on the one hand, and saying that it is the *function* of the heart to pump blood, on the other. The functional attribution introduces normativity. For example, we can now talk about better and worse hearts, heart disease, and so on. The normativity is a consequence of the fact that the functional attribution situates the causal facts within a teleology. The attribution of function presupposes the notion of a purpose, or a goal, or an objective, and thus the attribution ascribes more than just causal relations. These purposes, goals, and objectives exist only relative to human and animal agents. It is only because we value life and survival and we understand the contribution of the heart to life and survival that we can say that the *function* of the heart is to pump blood. If we valued death and extinction above all, then hearts would be dysfunctional, and the function of disease would be to hasten extinction. We can summarize the general point by saying that all functions are observer-relative. Functions are never observer-independent. Causation is observer-independent; what function adds to causation is normativity or teleology. More precisely, the attribution of function to causal relations situates the causal relations within a presupposed teleology.

Constitutive Rules

I have all along been talking as if we had a satisfactory notion of an institutional reality in addition to a brute reality, but we need to state some of the presuppositions of that assumption.

Years ago I made a distinction between brute facts, such as the fact that the sun is ninety-three million miles from the earth, and institutional facts, such as the fact that I am a citizen of the United States. In order to account for the distinction between brute facts and institutional facts, I appealed to a distinction between two different kinds of rules. Some rules regulate antecedently existing forms of behavior. Think, for example, of the rule "Drive on the right-hand side of the road." Driving can exist on either side of the road, but given the fact of driving, it is useful to have some way of regulating it, and so we have rules of the form "Do this or do that." And in general we have rules that regulate activities that exist independently of the rules. Such rules are regulative. They regulate antecedently existing forms of behavior. But not all rules are of that sort. Some rules not only regulate but also constitute, or make possible, the form of activity that they regulate. The classic example is the rules of chess. It is not the case that people were pushing bits of wood around on a board and someone finally said, "In order to keep from banging into each other, we need to get some rules." The rules of chess are not like the rules of driving. Rather, the very possibility of playing chess depends on there being rules of chess, because playing chess consists in acting in accordance with at least a certain sizable subset of the rules of chess. Such rules I call "constitutive rules," because acting in accord with the rules is constitutive of the activity regulated by the rules. Constitutive rules also regulate, but they do more than regulate; they constitute the very activity that they regulate in the way that I have suggested. The distinction between brute facts and institutional facts, I have argued and will continue to argue here, can only be fully explained in terms of constitutive rules, because institutional facts only exist within systems of such rules.

Constitutive rules always have the same logical form, even in cases where the logical form is not obvious from the grammar of the sentences expressing the rule. They are always of the logical form: such-and-such counts as having the status so-and-so. I like to put this in the form "X counts as Y," or more generally, "X counts as Y in (context) C." Thus, in the context of a chess game, such-and-such a move on the part of a certain shape of piece counts as a move by the knight. Such-and-such a position on the board counts as a checkmate. In American football, to cross the opponent's goal line in possession of the ball while a play is in progress counts as scoring a touchdown. A touchdown counts as six points. Getting more points than the opposition counts as winning.

A Simple Model of the Construction of Institutional Reality

In this chapter, I am making a very strong claim: all of institutional reality can be explained using exactly these three notions, collective intentionality, the assignment of function, and constitutive rules. In order to substantiate this claim I want to begin with a simple thought experiment, a kind of parable as to how creatures like ourselves might have evolved institutional structures. Imagine a group of primitive creatures more or less like ourselves. It is easy to imagine that they individually assign functions to natural objects. For example, an individual might use this stump as a seat and that stick as a lever. And if an individual can assign functions using individual intentionality, it is not hard to imagine that several individuals can assign functions collectively. A group can use this log as a bench and that big stick as a lever to be manipulated by all of them. Now imagine that, acting as a group, they build a barrier, a wall around the place where they live. I don't want to call the place where they live a "village," or even a "community," because those terms might seem already too institutional. But these individuals, we will suppose, do have shelters—even caves would do—and we suppose they build a wall around the area of their shelters.

The wall is designed to keep intruders out and keep members of the group in.

The wall has an assigned function in virtue of its physical features. We suppose that the wall is too big to climb over easily and that the inhabitants of the shelters can easily stop such climbing. Notice that the wall, as so far described, has two of the features that we mentioned earlier as essential to institutional reality. It has both the assignment of function and collective intentionality. A function has been assigned to the wall—the function of acting as a boundary barrier—by the inhabitants acting collectively. The wall, we are supposing, was constructed as a cooperative effort by them in order to perform its function. Now, to these features I want to add the third. I want to vary the story slightly in a way that I hope will sound innocent even though an enormous set of issues depends on it. Let us suppose that the wall gradually decays. It slowly deteriorates until all that is left is a line of stones. But let us suppose that the inhabitants continue to treat the line of stones as if it could perform the function of the wall. Let us suppose that, as a matter of fact, they treat the line of stones just as if they understood that it was not to be crossed. Of course, we must not suppose that they have any concepts as grand as "duty" or "obligation," but we suppose that they understand that one is just not supposed to cross this line of stones.

Now, as I said, I want this story to sound innocent, but I believe that a very important shift has taken place with this addition. This shift is the decisive move in the creation of institutional reality. It is nothing less than the decisive move in the creation of what we think of as distinctive in human, as opposed to animal, societies. Here is why. Initially the wall performed its assigned function in virtue of its physical structure. But what has happened in the story, as I revised it, is that the wall now performs its function not in virtue of its physical structure but in virtue of the collective acceptance or recognition by the individuals acting collectively that the wall has a certain status and with that status goes a certain function. I want to introduce a term to describe the results of this transition. I call these functions "status functions."

I believe this move, the move from physics to the collective acceptance of a status function, forms the basic conceptual structure behind human institutional reality. It is generally the case with institutional structures that the structure cannot perform its function in virtue of its physics alone but requires collective acceptance. Where human institutions are concerned, the functions, in short, are status functions.

The Example of Money

Perhaps the clearest case of this phenomenon is money. Money cannot perform its functions in virtue of physics alone. No matter how much by way of function we try to assign to the physics, the physics of money alone—unlike the physics of a knife or a bathtub—does not enable the performance of the function. For functions that are not status functions, such as the functions of a bathtub or a knife, the physics is essential to the performance of the function. The physical structure enables me to use my bathtub as a bathtub but not as a knife, and it enables me to use my knife as a knife but not as a bathtub. With status functions, however, there is a break between the physics of the system, on the one hand, and the status and the functions that go along with that status, on the other.

We can illustrate these points by considering some features of the evolution of paper currency in Western Europe. It is standard in economics textbooks to say that there are three types of money. The first type is "commodity money," which is the use of a commodity that is regarded as valuable as a kind of money. A system of commodity money is essentially a system of barter. The second sort of money is "contract money." Such money consists of contracts to pay the bearer with something valuable on demand. The third sort of money is "fiat money." Fiat money is money only in virtue of the fact that it has been declared to be money, by fiat, by some powerful agency. The puzzle is, what is it that all these have in common that makes them all money, and how does each work?

In the evolution of currency, the first stage was to have valuable commodities, typically gold and silver, which could be used as a medium of exchange and as a store of value. The gold and silver are not intrinsically valuable. The possession of "value" is an imposed function, but in this case, the function is imposed in virtue of the physical features of the object in question. And indeed, in the early days of gold and silver coinage, the value of the coin was exactly equal to the amount of the gold and silver in it. Governments sometimes cheated, but in principle, that was the idea. If you melted down the coin, it did not lose any of its value. The printing on the coin was just a way of identifying how much it was worth by indicating the amount of gold or silver in it.

However, carrying gold and silver around is a rather inefficient way to conduct business, and it is also rather dangerous. So, in Europe in the Middle Ages, possessors of gold and silver found it was safer to keep the gold and silver with a "banker." The banker would give them bits of paper or other sorts of documents on which it was written that the documents could be redeemed in gold or silver on demand. We thus have a move from commodity money to contract money. A piece of paper that substitutes for the gold is now a contract to pay the bearer. At some point, some genius discovered that you could increase the supply of money in the economy by issuing more contracts than you actually have gold or silver, and as long as not everybody runs to the banker at once, demanding their gold or silver, the system continues to work just as well as before the change from commodity money to contract money. The bits of paper, as they say, are as good as gold, or, for that matter, silver.

Finally, and this development took a long time, some later genius discovered that you could forget all about the gold and silver and just have the bits of paper. That is our present situation in the economically advanced nations. Many simple-minded people have the illusion that American currency is "backed by the gold in Fort Knox," but the notion of backing is quite illusory. What one has when one has a twenty-dollar bill, for example, is a bit of paper that functions in virtue of an imposed status function. The bill has no value as a commodity, and it has no value as a contract; it is a pure case of status function.

For a long time the Treasury allowed the illusion to persist that the piece of paper was still a contract. Thus, for instance, it said on the twenty-dollar Federal Reserve note that the Treasury would pay the bearer on demand the sum of twenty dollars. But if one had actually insisted on payment, the only thing that could have been forthcoming was equivalent currency, such as another twenty-dollar Federal Reserve note. The U.S. Treasury has now abandoned this hypocrisy, but the pretense still exists in Britain, where the twenty-pound note contains a promise by the governor of the Bank of England to pay the bearer on demand twenty pounds.

The main point I want to make with this discussion of the evolution of currency is that the move from commodity money to fiat money is a move from the assignment of a function in virtue of physical structure to a pure case of status function. The assignment of status function has the form "X counts as Y in C." Such-and-such patterned bits of paper, issued by the Bureau of Engraving and Printing, under the authority of the Treasury, simply *count as* money, that is, "Legal Tender for All Debts Public and Private," in the United States.

How Institutional Reality
Can Be So Powerful

So far, I have described a rather simple mechanism by which we have imposed status functions on entities in virtue of collective intentionality, following the general form "X counts as Y in C." Now, this must seem a very simple and fragile mechanism for the creation of institutional structures such as governments, armies, universities, banks, and so on, and even more fragile if we consider such general human institutions as private property, marriage, and political power. How can such a simple mechanism generate such a vast apparatus? I think the general form of the answer to that can be stated fairly simply. It involves two mechanisms. First, the structure "X counts as Y in C" can be *iterated*. You can pile one status function on top of another. The X term at one level may have been a Y term at an earlier level, and you can keep repeatedly turning Y terms into X terms that count as yet another Y on top of each other. Furthermore, in complex societies, the C term (context) is typically a Y term from an earlier stage. Let me give you some examples of how that works.

I make noises through my mouth. So far, that is a brute fact: there is nothing institutional about noises as such. But, as I am a speaker of English addressing other English speakers, those noises *count as* the utterance of an English sentence; they are an instance of the formula "X counts as Y in C." But now, in an utterance of that English sentence, the Y term from the previous level now functions as an X term at the next level. The utterance of that English sentence with those intentions and in that context counts as, for example, making a promise. But now that Y term, the promise, is the X term at the next level up. Making that sort of promise in those sorts of circumstances counts as undertaking a contract. Notice what I have done. I have taken the brute X term—I made the noises—and piled on further Y terms by the repeated application of the formula. Y_1 becomes X_2, which counts as Y_2, which becomes X_3, and so on, up until we reach the point where I made a contract. Furthermore, we can suppose that that sort of contract, in those sorts of circumstances, counts as getting married. And then, getting married in turn counts as qualifying for all sorts of benefits, obligations, rights, duties, and so on. This is one mechanism for using the apparatus to create complex social structures. You simply repeat, or iterate, the mechanism over and over. Furthermore, in many cases the C term—the context—is itself the product of some prior imposition of status function. So, for example, in the state of California you can get married only if you are in the presence of a qualified official. But being a qualified official, though it is a context C in the application of the rules for getting married, is itself the result of the imposition of a status function. The C term at one level is a Y term from another level. Some individual X was, under circumstance C, certified as the qualified official Y. To summarize this point, one mechanism for producing complex structures out of such a simple device is the repeated application of the device.

A second feature that is crucial in the real-life functioning of institutional structures is that institutional facts do not exist in isolation but in complex interrelations with each other. So, for example, I don't just have money. I have *money* earned as an *employee* of the *state of California*, and I have it in my *bank account*, which I use to pay my *state and federal taxes* as well as the *bills* owing to the *gas and electric companies* and to the *contractor of my credit cards*. Notice that in the previous sentence, all of the italicized expressions are institutional terms. They make reference to assorted interconnected, diverse forms of institutional reality. Thus, we are able to use this simple mechanism to create a fantastically rich social structure by interlocking operations of the mechanism and complex iterations of the mechanism, piling one on top of the other.

But it may all still seem very fragile. How is it possible that we can do so much with so little? The answer to that question, again, is very complex in detail but simple in its general form. The answer is that we do not have separate and mutually exclusive classes of brute and institutional facts. The whole point, or at least much of the point, of having institutional facts is to gain social control of the brute facts. Thus, in a recent exchange that I had, it is true that I gave the other people only bits of paper or showed them a piece of plastic, and they only made noises at me through their mouths and gave me other bits of paper, but the result is that, having exchanged the noises and the bits of paper, I could then get on an airplane and fly a long distance away—a brute change of my geographical location. Similarly, as a result of such status functions, I live in a house that I would not otherwise live in. More generally, because of the assignment of status functions, people are thrown in jail, or executed, or go to war. So, it would be a misunderstanding to suppose that there are separate, isolated classes of brute facts and institutional facts. On the contrary, we have complex interpenetrations of brute and institutional facts. Indeed, typically the purpose or the function of the institutional structure is to create and control brute facts. Institutional reality is a matter of positive and negative powers—including rights, entitlements, honor, and authority, as well as obligations, duties, disgrace, and penalties.

Solutions to the Problem and the Puzzles

With all this in mind, let us attempt to solve the main problem and the three puzzles that I mentioned in the beginning of this chapter.

The main problem was, how can there be an objective social and institutional reality that is the reality it is only because we think it is? The answer is that the collective assignment of status functions, and above all their continued recognition and acceptance over long periods of time, can create and maintain a reality of governments, money, nation-states, languages, ownership of private property, universities, political parties, and a thousand other such institutions that can seem as epistemically objective as geology and as much a permanent part of our landscape as rock formations. But with the withdrawal of collective acceptance, such institutions can collapse suddenly, as witness the amazing collapse of the Soviet empire in a matter of months, beginning in *annus mirabilus* 1989.

Now to our three puzzles.

First, what about self-referentiality? Do we not have the result that there is a self-referential paradox if it is part of the definition of money that it is believed to be money? I believe the paradox is not serious and is easily removed. It is true that we find it natural to say that part of being money is being believed to be money. But the word *money* does not function essentially in the definition of money. If something is regarded as and used as a medium of exchange, a store of value, a device for paying debts, and as valid tender generally, then it is money. We do not need the word *money* to state these facts. The word *money* is just a place-holder for a complex set of intentional activities, and it is the capacity for playing a role in those activities that constitutes the essence of money. In order to think that something is money, people do not need to use the word *money* itself; they can think that the entity in question is a medium of exchange, a store of value, a mechanism for paying debts or for services rendered, and so on.

Our second puzzle was, how can this socially created mechanism function causally? Can it actually have any causal effects? The answer was already hinted at by the remarks that I made earlier—namely, that collective acceptance is itself a mechanism for the creation of power. So, to take an obvious sort of case, if we collectively accept that someone is president of the United States, then as such he has an enormous amount of power. He can veto bills passed by Congress, he is in command of the U.S. armed forces, and he can perform a very large number of other acts of exercising power. Indeed, all of institutional reality in one way or another is about power: there are positive powers, such as the powers of the presidency, and there are negative powers, such as the duty of the citizens to pay taxes. There are conditional powers, such as the right of a baseball batter to advance to first base on the condition that he was pitched four balls, and there are honorific surrogates for power, as when one is awarded an honorary degree by a university.

Our third puzzle was, what is the role of language in the creation of institutional reality? One obvious but nonetheless puzzling use of language in the construction of institutional reality is that often we can create institutional facts by a performative utterance. We can hire somebody by saying, "You're hired." We can declare war by saying, "War is declared," and so on, for a very large number of cases. How is this possible? The answer is that often in our constitutive rules the X term is itself a speech act. Thus, when I say, "I hereby give and bequeath my car to my nephew," in an appropriate context, I am in fact giving and bequeathing my car to my nephew. Saying in the right context C, "War is declared," is declaring war. It is creating the institutional fact that a state of war exists between two countries. So, one role of language is fairly easily accounted for, and that is the use of performative utterances in the creation of institutional facts. The general point is that where the X term is a speech act, the performance of that speech act is performative in the sense that it creates the institutional fact named by the Y term.

But that still does not answer the deeper question: Why is it that we feel in general that language plays a different role in institutional reality from what it plays in brute physical reality? How is it that in institutional reality we use language not only to describe but partly to create the very facts described? The answer that I will propose depends on the fact that the symbolizing aspect of language is essential to the constitution of institutional reality in a way that is not essential to brute reality, because the move whereby we agree to count an X term as having the status Y is already a symbolizing move. We discuss this issue in greater detail in the next chapter.

In our effort to give an account of our situation, here is how far we have come: there is a reality that exists totally independently of us, an observer-independent way that things are, and our statements about that reality are true or false depending on whether they accurately represent how things are.

That reality consists of physical particles in fields of force. The particles are typically organized into larger systems. One such system is our little solar system, including our home planet as a subsystem. On our planet certain systems mostly composed of carbon-based molecules are living systems that are members of species that have evolved over long periods of time. Some of those living systems are animals, some animals have nervous systems, and some nervous systems can cause and sustain consciousness. Conscious animals typically have intentionality.

Once a species is capable of consciousness and intentionality, collective intentionality is not a very large step. My guess is that all conscious, intentionalistic animal species have some form of collective intentionality, but I do not know enough ethology and animal biology for that to be more than a guess. With collective intentionality a species automatically has social facts and social reality.

Consciousness and intentionality are observer-independent real parts of the real world, but they give animals the capacity to create observer-relative phenomena. Among these observer-relative phenomena are functions. Many species have the capacity to assign functions to objects. A capacity that is apparently unique to humans is the ability to impose status functions and thus to create institutional facts. Status functions require language or at least a language-like capacity for symbolization.

SIX

How Language Works: Speech as a Kind of Human Action

In earlier chapters, we discussed some astounding phenomena. One of these was the existence of consciousness in a world composed entirely of physical particles. Another was the remarkable capacity of the mind to direct itself at objects and states of affairs in the world apart from itself. A third was the ability of minds, acting in cooperation, to create an objective social reality. In this chapter, we discuss an equally amazing phenomenon, the existence of human linguistic communication.

Perhaps the simplest way to call attention to the astounding character of language is to remind ourselves of the following fact: in the lower portion of your face and mine is a cavity that opens by way of a hinged flap. Periodically, that cavity opens and varieties of noises come out. For the most part, these noises are caused by the passage of air over mucous-covered cords in the larynx. From a purely physical point of view, the acoustic blasts produced by these physical and physiological phenomena are fairly trivial. However, they have remarkable features. An acoustic blast that comes out of my mouth can be said to be a statement, a question, an explanation, a command, an exhortation, an order, a promise, and so on, or a very large number of other possibilities. Furthermore, what comes out can be said to be true or false or boring or uninteresting or exciting or original or stupid or simply irrelevant. Now, the remarkable thing is that we get from the acoustic blast to these amazing semantic properties, which include not only rhetorical and linguistic phenomena but even political, literary, and other sorts of cultural phenomena. How does it work? How do we get from the physics to the semantics? That is the question I discuss in this chapter.

Speech Acts: Illocutionary Acts and Perlocutionary Acts

Whenever I emit one of these acoustic blasts in a normal speech situation, I can be said to have performed a *speech act*. Speech acts come in a variety of types. By means of these acoustical blasts, I make a statement or ask a question, I give an order or make a request, or I explain some scientific problem or predict an event in the future. All of these, and dozens of other examples like them, were baptized by the British philosopher J. L. Austin as "illocutionary acts." The illocutionary act is the minimal complete unit of human linguistic communication. Whenever we talk or write to each other, we are performing illocutionary acts.[1]

We need to distinguish illocutionary acts, which are the target of our analysis proper, from the effects or consequences that illocutionary acts have on hearers. So, for example, by *ordering* you to do something, I might *get you to do it*. By *arguing* with you, I might *persuade* you. In making a statement, I might *convince* you, by *recounting* a story, I might *amuse* you. In these examples, the first of each pair of verbs mentions an illocutionary act or acts, but the second verb phrase mentions the effect that the illocutionary act has on a hearer, an effect such as persuading, convincing, and getting someone to do something. Austin, the inventor of this terminology, baptized these acts that have to do with further consequences beyond linguistic communication as "perlocutionary acts." So, our first distinction is between the illocutionary act, which is the real target of our analysis, and the perlocutionary act, which has to do with further consequences or effects of our actions, whether illocutionary acts or otherwise, on hearers. Typically, illocutionary acts have to be performed intentionally. If you did not intend to make a promise or a statement, then you did not make a promise or a statement. But perlocutionary acts do not have to be performed intentionally. You might persuade somebody of something, or get them to do something, or annoy them, or amuse them, without intending to do so. The fact that illocutionary acts are essentially intentional, whereas perlocutionary acts may or may not be intentional, is a consequence of the fact that the illocutionary act is the unit of *meaning* in communication. When the speaker says something, and means something by what he says, and tries to communicate what he means to a hearer, he will, if successful, have performed an illocutionary act. Illocutionary acts, meaning, and intention are all tied together in ways that I explain in this chapter.

In addition to the distinction between illocutionary and perlocutionary acts, we also need a distinction within the illocutionary act between the content of the act and the type of act it is. This distinction is exactly parallel to the distinction we made in chapter 4 between the propositional content of an intentional state and the type of intentional state it is. To take an obvious example, consider the differences between utterances of these sentences:

Please leave the room.
Will you leave the room?
You will leave the room.

These utterances have something in common, namely, each contains an expression of the proposition that you will leave the room. In each utterance, there is something different from the other utterances. The first is a request, the second a question, the third a prediction. Parallel to the distinction in our theory of intentionality between the content of the intentional state and the type of intentional state it is, we need a distinction between the content of an illocutionary act and the illocutionary *force* it has or—what is the same thing—the type of illocutionary act it is. For purposes of our analysis, we can represent the structure of illocutionary acts as $F(p)$, where F stands for illocutionary force and p for propositional content. That is, we can separate the part of the speech act that constitutes its illocutionary type or illocutionary force from the part that constitutes its propositional content.

With all this in mind, we have now isolated our target of analysis a little more accurately than we had at the beginning of this chapter. The question now is this: How do we get from the sounds we make to the illocutionary act? At first sight, that question might seem to be different from the traditional questions that form the basis of the philosophy of language. The traditional questions are: "How does language relate to reality?" and "What is meaning?" But I think that, at bottom, my question and the traditional questions are the same, because the question "How do you get from the sound to the type of illocutionary act?" is really the same question as "How does the mind bestow meaning on mere marks and sounds?" And the answer to that question will give us an analysis of the concept of meaning that we can use to explain how language relates to reality. Language relates to reality in virtue of meaning, but meaning is the property that turns mere utterances into illocutionary acts. Illocutionary acts are meaningful in a very special sense of the word, and it is that type of meaningfulness that enables language to relate to reality. So, at bottom, appropriately understood, the three questions "What is meaning?" "How does language relate to reality?" and "What is the nature of the illocutionary act?" are the same question. As we will see, all three questions are concerned with how the mind imposes intentionality on sounds and marks, thereby conferring meanings upon them and, in so doing, relating them to reality.

The Meanings of "Meaning"

Notoriously, the words *mean, meaning, meaningful,* and so on, are ambiguous in English. Think of the occurrence of these expressions in the following sentences:

1. You mean a lot to me, Mabel.
2. Life became meaningless after the Republican defeat.
3. The meaning of historical events is seldom apparent at the time of the event.
4. I didn't mean to hurt you.
5. The German sentence "Es regnet" means "It's raining."
6. When Friedrich said, "Es regnet," he meant, "It's raining."

I will not say anything about the senses of "meaning" in the first four sentences except to say that they are not the senses that are essential for understanding *meaning* in the linguistic sense. For the purposes of our investigation, I want to zero in on sentences 5 and 6, because they exemplify the types of meaning that I am most concerned with in this chapter.

It is customary and correct to describe the type of distinction between sentences 5 and 6 as the distinction between *sentence meaning* or *word meaning*, on the one hand, and *speaker meaning* or *utterance meaning*, on the other hand. Sentences and words have meanings as parts of a language. The meaning of a sentence is determined by the meanings of the words and the syntactical arrangement of the words in the sentence. But what the speaker *means by the utterance* of the sentence is, within certain limits, entirely a matter of his or her intentions. I have to say "within certain limits" because you can't just say anything and mean anything. You can't say, "Two plus two equals four" and mean that Shakespeare was a pretty good poet as well as a playwright. At least you can't mean that without a lot of extra stage setting. The meaning of the sentence is entirely a matter of the conventions of the language. But sentences are tools to talk with. So even though language constrains speaker meaning, speaker meaning is still the primary form of linguistic meaning, because the linguistic meaning of sentences functions to enable speakers of the language to use sentences to mean something in utterances. The speaker's utterance meaning is the primary notion of meaning for our purposes in analyzing the functions of language.

In the rest of this chapter, when I examine the question "What is meaning?" I will be addressing the question "What is speaker meaning?" In light of the discussion in the earlier part of this chapter, that question can now be rephrased as "How is it that speakers can impose meaning on mere sounds made from their mouths or on marks made on paper?"

This may appear to be a rather innocent question, but in fact there is a *huge* and apparently endless debate in the philosophical tradition on precisely this issue. I would not wish to give the reader the impression that somehow the

question is easy or that my answer is uncontroversial. However, I am, for present purposes, going to cut through all the
traditional debates and give what I think is the correct answer to the question straight out, just like that.

The key to understanding meaning is this: meaning is a
form of derived intentionality. The original or intrinsic intentionality of a speaker's thought is transferred to words,
sentences, marks, symbols, and so on. If uttered meaningfully, those words, sentences, marks, and symbols now have
intentionality derived from the speaker's thoughts. They
have not just conventional linguistic meaning but intended
speaker meaning as well. The conventional intentionality of
the words and sentences of a language can be used by a
speaker to perform a speech act. When a speaker performs a
speech act, he imposes his intentionality on those symbols.
How exactly does he do that? We saw earlier in our discussion of intentionality that conditions of satisfaction, in a
sense I tried to explain, are the key to understanding intentionality. Intentional phenomena, such as fears, hopes, desires, beliefs, and intentions, have conditions of satisfaction.
Hence, when a speaker says something and means something, he is performing an intentional act, and his production
of the sounds is part of the conditions of satisfaction of his
intention in making the utterance. But when he makes a
meaningful utterance, he imposes conditions of satisfaction
on those sounds and marks. In making a meaningful utterance, he thus *imposes conditions of satisfaction on conditions of satisfaction*.

This is the essential feature of meaning, and I will explain
it in more detail. Suppose, for example, that a German
speaker, Friedrich, intentionally says, "Es regnet," and
means it. He will have performed a complex act with several
conditions of satisfaction. First, he intended to utter the sentence, and that utterance was the condition of satisfaction of
this part of his complex intention. But, second, because he
not only intended to utter the sentence but meant it, that is,

he meant that it is raining, the utterance acquired conditions of satisfaction of its own. The utterance will be satisfied if and only if it is raining. The conditions of satisfaction of the utterance are truth conditions. The utterance will be true or false depending on whether the world is as Friedrich intentionally represents it as being when he makes the utterance. So Friedrich had at least two parts to his intention: the intention to make the utterance and the intention that the utterance should have certain conditions of satisfaction. But since the utterance is the condition of satisfaction of the first part of his intention, his whole meaning intention was the intention to impose conditions of satisfaction on conditions of satisfaction. Furthermore, if he was intending to communicate to a hearer, he would have had a third part to his intention in the performance of the speech act, the intention that the hearer should understand him as stating that it is raining. But that third intention, the communicative intention, was just the intention that his first two intentions should be recognized by the hearer. The conditions of satisfaction of the communication intention are that the hearer should recognize that he uttered the sentence intentionally and that it has the conditions of satisfaction that the speaker intentionally imposed on it. I will say more about communication in the next section.

The discussion of meaning is the key issue for the present chapter, and in order to make the position fully clear, I want to go through the problem step by step with another example. Suppose that I am learning German. Suppose that I frequently practice saying in the shower, or while walking out on rainy days, "Es regnet, es regnet, es regnet." In such a case, I am just practicing my pronunciation; I don't actually *mean* that it is raining. So what is the difference between saying something and meaning it, on the one hand, and saying it and not meaning it, on the other? If we recall our slogan from chapter 4, we should look at the conditions of satisfaction. We would find that the conditions of satisfaction of the two intentions, saying and meaning, are quite different. The conditions of satisfaction of my intention when I say something without meaning it are simply that my intention should cause an utterance of a certain sort, a sort that conforms to the pronunciation rules of German. But what are the conditions of satisfaction of my intention when I actually mean what I say?

Suppose that I have actually learned a little German and someone asks me a question which I know means "What is the weather like today?"—"Wie ist das Wetter heute?" And I respond: "Es regnet." Now, I have the same intention that I had before to produce an utterance of a German sentence, but I also have a meaning intention. What is the meaning intention? Our natural temptation is to say that the meaning intention is that it actually be the case that it is raining when I utter the sentence "Es regnet." But that is not quite correct, because it is possible to say something and mean what one says and still be insincere. It is possible, in short, to lie. So, we need an account of meaning intentions that shows how I can say something and mean it, where my meaning intention can be the same whether I am lying or sincere.

In our account of intentionality, we saw that intentional states have conditions of satisfaction. The meaning intention is the intention that one's utterance should have additional conditions of satisfaction. But since the utterance is itself the condition of satisfaction of the intention to make the utterance, the meaning intention amounts to the intention that the conditions of satisfaction, that is, the utterance itself, should have conditions of satisfaction, that is, in this case, truth conditions. What I intend when I say, "Es regnet," and mean it, is that my utterance "Es regnet" should have truth conditions—and thus, when I say it and mean it, I am committed to its truth. This point holds whether I am lying or not. Both the liar and the truth teller make a commitment to tell the truth. The difference is that the liar is not keeping his commitment. So, the meaning intention amounts to the intention that when I say, "Es regnet," in addition to the condition of satisfaction of my intention to produce that utterance, the utterance itself now has conditions of satisfaction. When I say something and mean it, I am committed to the truth of what I say. And this is so whether I am sincere or insincere.

Meaning and Communication

I have so far talked mostly about the meaning intention. But of course, if I am actually answering a question about the weather, I intend more than that my utterance should be meaningful in the sense of having truth conditions and other conditions of satisfaction. If I am answering a question, I intend to communicate an answer to the hearer. The intention to speak meaningfully in words should not be confused with the intention to communicate that meaning to a hearer. Normally, the whole point of speaking is to communicate to a hearer, but the intention to communicate is not identical with the meaning intention—the intention that one's utterance should have truth conditions or other conditions of satisfaction.

What, then, is the intention to communicate? In answering this question, I will borrow and revise some ideas from Paul Grice.[2] Grice saw correctly that when we communicate to people, we succeed in producing understanding in them by getting them to recognize our intention to produce that understanding. Communication is peculiar among human actions in that we succeed in producing an intended effect on the hearer by getting the hearer to recognize the intention to produce that very effect. This is not generally the case with human action. We do not generally succeed in our actions just by getting other people to recognize what we are trying to do. I cannot, for example, win a race or become president of the United States just by getting people to recognize my intention to win the race or to become president. But when I am trying to tell someone that it is raining, I succeed in telling them as soon as they recognize that I am trying to tell them something and what exactly it is that I am trying to tell them. I can, for example, tell them that it is raining just by getting them to recognize my intention to tell them that it is raining.

How does it work? When I intend to communicate, I intend to produce understanding. But understanding will consist in the grasp of my meaning. Thus, the intention to communicate is the intention that the hearer should recognize my meaning, that is, understand me. But what that amounts to in my saying "Es regnet" and meaning it and intending to communicate to a hearer that it is raining, is the intention that the hearer should recognize my meaning intention. The communication intention is the intention to produce in the hearer the knowledge of my meaning by getting him to recognize my intention to produce in him that knowledge. Thus, going through the steps of the utterance of "Es regnet," my speaker's meaning and my communication intention amount to the following: I utter the sentence "Es regnet" with the intentions that

1. I should be correctly uttering a sentence of German with its conventional meaning;
2. my utterance should have conditions of satisfaction, namely, the truth condition that it is raining; and
3. the hearer should recognize intention 2, and he should recognize intention 2 by means of his recognition of intention 1 and his knowledge of the conventions of German.

If the hearer does recognize intentions 1 and 2, I will have succeeded in achieving intention 3. That is, if the hearer knows the language, recognizes my intention to produce a sentence of the language, and recognizes that I am not merely uttering that sentence but that I also mean what I say, then I will have succeeded in communicating to the hearer that it is raining.

Notice that this analysis is independent of the question of whether I am telling the truth or lying, whether I am sincere or insincere. I will have succeeded in making the statement that it is raining even if I am lying. This is a key point: even if I am lying, by saying something and meaning what I say, I am committed to the truth of what I say. So, I can have a commitment to the truth even if in fact I believe that what I say is false.

Various Types of Speech Acts

In the analysis of language I have presented, the basic unit is the speech act. I have given several examples of speech acts earlier in this chapter: statements, orders, promises, and so on. But that raises the question of how many types of speech acts, how many types of illocutionary acts, are there? How many sorts of conditions of satisfaction can we impose on conditions of satisfaction? Language has an enormous variety of uses. We can make up jokes, tell stories, give instructions and recipes, produce involved scientific explanations or mathematical formulae, or write poems or works of fiction. However, it seems to me that in the illocutionary act line of business, there is a restricted number of things we can do. Because, as we saw, the structure of the illocutionary act is $F(p)$, where the F marks the illocutionary force and the p marks the propositional content, the question "How many types of illocutionary acts are there?" is the same question as "How many types of F are there?" The propositional content can be infinitely diverse, but we can, so to speak, factor it out because the same propositional content can occur in differ-ent types of illocutionary acts, as our previous discussion has shown. So now we have narrowed the question down to

"How many types of F are there?" It might seem that we could begin to answer it by looking at the different verbs that name illocutionary acts in English, verbs like *state, warn, command, promise, plead, pray, contract, guarantee, apologize,* and *complain.* But if we do this, we find a bewildering variety of verbs, which gives the impression of an enormous number of types of illocutionary acts.

One way to overcome this problem is to try to focus on certain common features. To do this, I need to introduce the notion of "illocutionary point." The illocutionary point of a speech act will be its point or purpose in virtue of its being an act of that type. Thus, for example, a person might give an order for a number of different reasons, and with a number of different degrees of urgency, but insofar as it is correctly described as an order, then, qua order, it *counts as* an attempt to get the hearer to do something. When a person makes a promise, he or she might make a promise for a variety of reasons, and with a variety of different degrees of strength. But insofar as it is a promise, then, qua promise, it *counts as* a commitment or an undertaking of an obligation by the speaker to do something for the hearer. The careful reader will notice that the locution "counts as," which we used so heavily in chapter 5, has reappeared in our discussion of illocutionary acts, and that is not an accident. The notion of illocutionary point is the notion of what an utterance counts as, as determined by the constitutive rules of speech acts. Thus, performing illocutionary acts is imposing a type of status function.

Furthermore, the illocutionary point of a speech act relates it to the theory of intentionality that we explained in chapter 4. The illocutionary point determines both the direction of fit and which intentional state is expressed in the performance of the speech act. Thus, for example, if I make a promise, then I necessarily express an intention to do the thing I promised to do. If I promise to come to your party, then I necessarily express an intention to come to your party.

That is, I express an intentional state with the same propositional content as the speech act itself, and that intentional state, that I intend to come to your party, is the sincerity condition on the speech act. So, just to summarize, the notion of illocutionary point automatically brings two other notions along with it—the notion of direction of fit and the notion of an intentional state that constitutes the sincerity condition on the speech act.

Now, let's go back and restate our question. "How many types of F are there, that is, how many types of illocutionary acts are there?" can be narrowed down to the question "How many types of illocutionary points are there?" If we take the notion of illocutionary point and its implied notions of an expressed sincerity condition and direction of fit as our basic tools of analysis, then it seems to me that there is a restricted number of things we can do by way of performing illocutionary acts and that these are determined by the structure of the mind. In a word, since the mind creates meaning by imposing conditions of satisfaction on conditions of satisfaction, then the limits to meaning are set by the limits of the mind. And what are those limits?

There are five and only five different types of illocutionary points:

1. First there is the *assertive* illocutionary point. The point of assertive speech acts is to commit the hearer to the truth of the proposition. It is to present the proposition as representing a state of affairs in the world. Some examples are statements, descriptions, classifications, and explanations. All assertives have the word-to-world direction of fit, and the sincerity condition of assertives is always belief. Every assertive is an expression of a belief. The simplest test for identifying assertives is to ask whether the utterance can be literally true or false. Because the assertives have the word-to-world direction of fit, they can be true or false.

2. The second illocutionary point is the *directive*. The illocutionary point of directives is to try to get the hearer to be-

have in such a way as to make his behavior match the propositional content of the directive. Examples of directives are orders, commands, and requests. The direction of fit is always world-to-word, and the expressed psychological sincerity condition is always desire. Every directive is an expression of a desire that the hearer should do the directed act. Directives such as orders and requests cannot be true or false, but they can be obeyed, disobeyed, complied with, granted, denied, and so on.

3. The third illocutionary point is *commissive*. Every commissive is a commitment by the speaker to undertake the course of action represented in the propositional content. Examples of commissives are promises, vows, pledges, contracts, and guarantees. A threat is also a commissive, but unlike the other examples, it is against the interest of the hearer and not for the benefit of the hearer. The direction of fit of commissives is always world-to-word, and the expressed sincerity condition is always intention. Every promise or threat, for example, is an expression of an intention to do something. Promises and vows, like orders and commands, cannot be true or false, but they can be carried out, kept, or broken.

4. The fourth type of illocutionary point is the *expressive*. The illocutionary point of the expressive is simply to express the sincerity condition of the speech act. Examples of expressives are apologies, thanks, congratulations, welcomes, and condolences. In expressives the propositional content typically has the null direction of fit, because the truth of the propositional content is simply taken for granted. If I say, "I apologize for hitting you," or, "Congratulations on winning the prize," I take it for granted that I hit you, or that you won the prize, so I assume or presuppose a match between propositional content and reality. But the sincerity condition of expressives varies with the type of expressive. Thus, an apology is sincere if the speaker genuinely feels sorry about what he is apologizing for. Congratulations are sincere if the speaker genuinely feels glad about what he is congratulating the hearer for.

5. The final type of illocutionary point is that of *declarations*. In a declaration, the illocutionary point is to bring about a change in the world by representing it as having been changed. Performatives as well as other declarations create a state of affairs just by representing it as created. The favorite examples are utterances like "I pronounce you man and wife," "War is hereby declared," "You are fired," and "I resign." In these cases, we have the double direction of fit because we change the world and thus achieve the world-to-word direction of fit by representing it as having been changed, and thus achieve the word-to-world direction of fit. Declarations are unique among speech acts in that they actually make changes in the world solely in virtue of the successful performance of the speech act. If I successfully pronounce you man and wife, or declare war, then a state of affairs exists in the world that did not exist before. In general, such declarations are possible only because of the existence of extralinguistic institutions of the sort that we described in chapter 5.

Notice that one can perform a speech act of one of the other types, such as promising or ordering, by simply declaring that one is performing it. Thus, in the performative utterance "I promise to come and see you," the speaker first performs a declaration. He makes it the case by declaration that he is promising. However, in virtue of that fact, his utterance creates a promise. Since his saying "I promise" creates the state of affairs that it represents, that is, the state of affairs of the speaker promising, it constitutes both a promise and an assertion to the effect that it is a promise. So, it has all three types of illocutionary point—declarational, commissive, and assertive.

Not all speech acts are performed by uttering sentences whose literal meaning expresses the intended speaker meaning. One can request someone to pass the salt by saying literally, "I request you to pass the salt," or, "Pass the salt," but more commonly one says, "Can you pass the salt?", "Could you pass the salt?", "I would like the salt," "Would you pass the salt?", "Can you reach the salt?", and so on. Such cases, where one performs one speech act indirectly by performing another directly, are called "indirect speech acts." Other sorts of cases where sentence meaning differs systematically from intended speaker meaning include metaphor, metonymy, irony, sarcasm, hyperbole, and understatement.

All of these types of illocutionary acts are already prefigured in our discussion of intentionality. The limits of meaning are the limits of intentionality, and it is a consequence of our analysis of intentionality that there is a limited number of things you can do with language. There are only three directions of fit in our analysis of intentionality—mind-to-world, which is characteristic of assertives, world-to-mind, which is characteristic of directives and commissives, and the null case, which is characteristic of expressives. Why then do we have two different types of speech acts for one direction of fit—the world-to-word? We could decide to lump promises and orders together. We could think of a promise as an order one gives to oneself, and an order as a promise imposed on the hearer. However, the obligation undertaken by the speaker in the commissive is so special, and the speaker and the hearer are so important in the whole speech act situation in general, that I find it useful to distinguish between the hearer-based world-to-word direction of fit and the speaker-based world-to-word direction of fit. Also, language creates a possibility that individual human minds by themselves do not have, and that is the possibility of combining both directions of fit in the performance of the declaration. We cannot create a state of affairs by thinking it, but given our analysis of institutional reality in the previous chapter, we can see how it is possible to create institutional reality by way of the performative utterance. We can create a state of affairs by representing it as having been created. This combines both the word-to-world and world-to-word directions of fit. For example, if the chairperson of the meeting says, "The meeting is adjourned," that very utterance creates the state of affairs that the meeting is adjourned by representing it as being the case that the meeting is adjourned. More grandly, when Congress declares war, that body makes it the case that a state of war exists simply by saying that war exists.

So, I believe, suitably understood, our analysis of intentionality shows the possibilities and the limitations of language.

Constitutive Rules and Symbolism

I have all along been talking as if intentionality were one thing and language another, but of course, for real human beings, the possibilities of our intentionality are expanded enormously by acquiring a language. Animals and prelinguistic children can have primitive forms of intentionality. They can have beliefs, desires, perceptions, and intentions. But once the child begins to acquire language, the capacities of his intentionality increase enormously, and by a kind of boot-strapping effect, increased intentionality increases understanding of language, which leads to greater increase in intentionality. Any textbook on psycholinguistic child development illustrates this phenomenon. What we have, in effect, is not just the mind on one side and language on the other, but mind and language enriching each other until, for adult human beings, the mind is linguistically structured.

We should not assume that speakers simply have thoughts and then proceed to put them into words. That is a gross oversimplification. For all but the simplest thoughts, one has to have a language to think the thought. I can, without words, believe that it is raining or feel hungry, but I cannot believe that it will rain more frequently next year than it did this year, or that my hunger is caused by a sugar deficiency rather than an actual absence of food in my system, without words or equivalent symbolic devices with which to think these thoughts. The child develops the capacities to think and to speak hand in hand. How? The child starts with simple prelinguistic intentionality. It then learns a simple vocabulary that enables it to have a richer intentionality, which in turn enables a richer vocabulary, which in turn enables a richer intentionality—and so on up in a boot-strapping process. For all but the simplest thoughts, the child requires a language to think the thought, and for all but the simplest speech acts, the child requires a conventional language with sentences that have conventional sentence meanings in order to perform the speech act.

Both the imposition of a conventional meaning on words as well as the imposition of speaker meaning in the performance of a speech act are cases of the imposition of status functions in the sense that I explained in the last chapter. In both word meaning and speaker meaning, the users of the language impose a function on a physical phenomenon, whether a word type or an acoustic blast. They do this by imposing a status function according to the formula "X counts as Y in C." Both the conventional meaning of the words in the sentence "It's raining" and the speaker meaning in a particular situation whereby the speaker utters the sentence and means by it that it is raining, are cases of status function.

This fact, that language is also a matter of institutional facts, will make it sound as if language is just one more human institution among others. But language is special in ways we need to explain. I promised at the end of chapter 5 that I would explain the special role of language in the constitution of institutional facts. I believe that language is the fundamental human institution in the sense that other institutions, such as money, government, private property, marriage, and games, require language, or at least language-like forms of symbolism, in a way that language does not require the other institutions for its existence.

There are many features of language, such as the existence of modal auxiliary verbs, and the infinite generative capacity of syntax, which are not the phenomena that I am discussing now. I am now discussing a very special characteristic of language, which I call "symbolization." Humans have the capacity to use one object to stand for, represent, express, or symbolize something else. It is this basic symbolizing feature of language that I take to be an essential presupposition of institutional facts.

Here is the argument for that claim. It is part of the definition of status functions that the function cannot be performed solely in virtue of the physical features of the object that has the status function. The knife and the chair can perform their respective physical functions just in virtue of their physics, but the person or the piece of paper cannot perform the status functions of president or money just in virtue of the physics of the human body or the paper. Status functions can be performed only in virtue of the collective acceptance or recognition of something as having that function. But if that is so, then the agents involved in the collective acceptance or recognition must have some way to represent to themselves the fact that the object has the status function. Why? Because there is no way to read off the status function Y just from the physics of the X. For knives and chairs, their capacity to perform the function of knives and chairs is built into the physics, but for money and presidents, there is nothing there to the object X except its features as an object of the X sort. The only way to get to the Y status function is to represent the X object as having that status.

Typically we represent the status function with words. We have to be able to think, "This is money," or, "He is the president." But we do not wish to say that every status function must be represented in actual words of actual languages, because of course meaningful words are themselves objects with status functions, and we need to allow that words can have meanings without having to have other words with which we represent those original meanings. Otherwise, we would get a vicious infinite regress. Furthermore, there may be status functions possessed by cultures that have not evolved full-blown human languages. In such cases, the X term itself is used to symbolize the Y status. Now, and this is the crucial point, *to the extent that we use the X term to represent the Y status, we are using it symbolically, we are using it as a linguistic device.*

Consider, for example, the line of stones that functions as a boundary. The line of stones is an indexical symbol of the boundary. And by "indexical" I just mean that the stones represent the feature by their very presence. They represent the boundary by being at the boundary. The line of stones functions as a linguistic device because it stands for or represents the status function of the boundary. Analogously, words perform the function of meaning by expressing their meanings.

The sense then in which symbolization in this broad linguistic sense is essential to all institutional facts is that the move from X to Y in the formula X counts as Y in C is already a symbolizing move. The status function Y can be represented by some outside symbolic devices, as when we think, in words, "This is my property," or, "This is a five-dollar bill." In the limiting case, we can use the X object itself to represent the Y status function, as in the case of the line of stones symbolizing the boundary.

It is important to make absolutely clear what I am saying and what I am not saying. I am *not* saying that all of institutional reality is somehow textual or meaningful in the way that sentences and speech acts are meaningful. That would be a mistake. Sentences and speech acts are meaningful in the strict sense that they have a semantics. They have truth conditions or other sorts of conditions of satisfaction. Meaning for speech acts, as we have seen, is a matter of imposing conditions of satisfaction on conditions of satisfaction. But money and presidents are not in that way meaningful because they have as such no conditions of satisfaction. Meaning in the strict semantic, intentional sense is a special feature of certain sorts of institutional devices such as sentences and speech acts, as well as maps, graphs, and diagrams. But it is by no means universal.

What I *am* saying is that the move that imposes status functions on an X term is essentially a symbolizing move because the status function cannot lie in the physics of the X term alone. The X term can generate the Y status function only if we represent the X term as having that status function.

Another role of language in the functioning of institutional reality should be noted. Often we need some device to enable us to recognize an object as having a status function, even though the status is invisible in the object itself. For this purpose, we use what I call "status indicators." Obvious examples are wedding rings, uniforms, badges, passports, and driver's licenses. All of these are linguistic, even though not all use words. They are indeed all speech acts in the sense I have explained, because they have conditions of satisfaction. Wearing a wedding ring or a police uniform is a standing speech act that says, "I am married," or, "I am a member of the police force."

*   *   *

I described this book in chapter 1 as an attempt to make a modest contribution to the intellectual project of the Enlightenment vision. This book is an attempt to explain certain structural features of mind, language, and social reality and to explain the relations of logical dependency among them. I have now completed that attempt. The book proceeds from the assumption that we live in one world and that, within the limits set by our evolutionary endowments, that world is intelligible to us. I will not in this concluding section attempt to summarize what I have said, because the entire book is in large part already a summary of some of the ideas I have developed elsewhere over the past four decades.

Specialists in the various subjects I have discussed will feel that I have left out much of what is at the center of research in their respective disciplines. They are quite right so to feel. I have written about the issues that seem to me the most important, and my sense of importance is often at variance with mainstream opinion. Nonspecialists will feel—or at least I hope they will feel—that there must be an enormous amount more to be said on these questions. I have indeed only scratched the surface of the massive areas I have discussed. For at least some more detailed discussion of these issues, I recommend to the reader the works cited in "Suggestions for Further Reading."

Among the many relevant issues that I have not discussed are those of rationality, human freedom, and social value. I think, in fact, that these are not three separate topics, but different aspects of the same topic. An implicit conception of rationality is contained in this book, one that differs from the standard conception of rationality in our philosophical tradition, and I hope to develop it in detail in another book.

I want to conclude this entire discussion with some reflections about the nature of philosophy and how it differs from other areas of inquiry. I do not, of course, think there is a sharp dividing line between philosophy and other disciplines. Indeed, I have sometimes been assured by qualified professionals that what I was doing in this or that book was not really philosophy but linguistics or cognitive science or something else.

Let us begin by contrasting philosophy and science. "Philosophy" and "science" do not name distinct subject matters in the way that "economic history," "chemistry," and "Romance philology" name distinct subject matters because, in principle at least, both philosophy and science are universal in subject matter. Both aim for knowledge and understanding. When knowledge becomes systematic, and especially when systematic knowledge becomes secure to the point that we are confident that it is knowledge as opposed to mere opinion, we are more inclined to call it "science" and less inclined to call it "philosophy." Much of philosophy is concerned with questions that we do not know how to answer in the systematic way that is characteristic of science, and many of the results of philosophy are efforts to revise questions to the point that they can become scientific questions. In this book, for example, I have been trying to do that with the problem of consciousness.

These relations between philosophy and science explain why science is always right and philosophy is always wrong, and why there is never any progress in philosophy. As soon as we are confident that we really have knowledge and understanding in some domain, we stop calling it "philosophy" and start calling it "science," and as soon as we make some definite progress, we think ourselves entitled to call it "scientific progress." Something like this has been happening to the study of speech acts in my intellectual lifetime. It is gradually becoming a part of the science of linguistics as we become more confident of our methods and our results.

Beginning in the seventeenth century, the area of scientific knowledge increased enormously as we developed systematic methods for the investigation of nature. This gave many thinkers the illusion that the methods of the natural sciences, especially physics and chemistry, might be generally applied to solve the problems that most perplex us. Such optimism turned out to be unjustified, and most of the philosophical problems that worried the Greek philosophers—problems about truth, justice, virtue, and the good life, for example— are still with us.

Philosophical questions and investigations tend to have three features. First, as we have just seen in our contrast between philosophy and science, much of philosophy is concerned with questions that we do not yet have an agreed-on method of answering. This is why sometimes the questions will cease to be philosophical when we find a method for answering them. A good example of this is the problem of the nature of life. This was once a philosophical problem, but it ceased to be so when advances in molecular biology enabled us to break down what seemed a large mystery into a series of smaller, manageable, specific biological questions and answers. I hope that something similar will happen to the problem of consciousness. The fact that philosophical questions tend to be those for which there is no generally accepted procedure of solution also explains why there is no agreed body of expert opinion in philosophy.

The fact that there are no universally accepted procedures for solving philosophical problems does not mean that anything goes, that you can say anything or that there are no standards. On the contrary, precisely the absence of such things as laboratory methods to fall back on forces the philosopher to even greater degrees of clarity, rigor, and precision. In philosophy there is no substitute for a combination of original, imaginative sensibility, on the one hand, and sheer intelligent, logical rigor on the other. The rigor without sensibility is empty, the sensibility without rigor is a lot of hot air.

A second feature of philosophical questions is that they tend to be what I call "framework" questions. That is, they tend to deal with the intellectual framework of our lives rather than the specific structures within the frameworks. So, for example, the question "What exactly is the cause of AIDS?" is not a philosophical question, but the question "What is the nature of causation?" is such a question. The former question is investigated within a framework where causation is taken for granted. The philosopher examines that framework. Again, the question "Is what Clinton says really true?" is not a philosophical question. But the question "What is truth?" is at the heart of philosophy.

A third feature of philosophical investigations is that they tend to be, in a broad sense, about conceptual issues. When we ask, in a philosophical tone of voice, what is truth, justice, virtue, or causation, we are not asking questions that can be answered just by having a good look at the environment or even by performing a good set of experiments on the environment. Such questions require at least in part an analysis of the concepts of "truth," "justice," "virtue," and "cause," and this means that the examination of language is an essential tool of the philosopher, because language is the vehicle for the articulation of our concepts.

It is no accident that these three features—unsolvability by universally accepted methods, frameworks as subject matter, and conceptual analysis as a first essential step in the investigation—tend to go together. Where we have ways of definitely solving problems, the solutions generally are found within already accepted frameworks where we take the conceptual apparatus for granted. Thus, in our earlier example, when we look for the cause of AIDS, we take for granted that we know what a disease is and what a cause is, and we have accepted methods for discovering the causes of diseases. We even have a general theory, the germ theory of disease, within which we conduct the investigation. But when we ask what causation is in general, we are scrutinizing a vast framework without any sure experimental methodology to guide us, and we have to begin by struggling with the ordinary concept of "cause" and its related family of concepts—"effect," "reason," "explanation," and so on.

In this book, I have been investigating the structure and interrelations of mind, language, and society—three interlocking frameworks. The methods are not those of the empirical sciences, where one would perform experiments or at least conduct public opinion surveys. The methods I employ are more adequately described, at least in the first stages, as logical or conceptual analysis. I try to find the constitutive elements of consciousness, intentionality, speech acts, and social institutions by taking them apart and seeing how they work. But, truth to tell, even that is a distortion of the actual methodology in practice. In practice, I use any weapon that I can lay my hands on, and I stick with any weapon that works. In studying the subjects of this book, for example, I read books ranging in subject matter from brain science to economics. Sometimes the results of the investigation are to reject the existing conceptual apparatus altogether. Thus, I claim we will not understand the relation of the mental to the physical as long as we continue to take seriously the old conceptual apparatus of dualism, monism, materialism, and all the rest of it. Here I am proposing a conceptual revision on the grounds that the old concepts are not adequate to the facts as we can now understand them, given a century of work on the brain. In other areas, the ontology of money or property, for example, we have to treat our ordinary concepts much more conservatively, because there is no underlying reality to socially created institutional reality except the capacity that human beings have to treat and regard certain phenomena in certain ways, and the conceptual apparatus is essential to that treatment and regard. But notice that such claims about what has to be rejected and what preserved come at the end and not the beginning of the investigation. So the claims themselves cannot provide methodological guidance in conducting the investigation.

The aim of philosophical analysis, as in any serious theoretical study, is to get a theoretical account of the problem areas that is at the same time true, explanatory, and general. In this book, I want not just to explain a lot of diverse phenomena but to show how they all hang together. Thus, my aim—not one shared by a majority of contemporary philosophers, by the way—has been to try to make progress toward getting an adequate *general* theory.

≡ NOTES

Introduction

1. John R. Searle, *Minds, Brains and Science* (Cambridge, Mass.: Harvard University Press, 1984).

Chapter 1

1. Gottlob Frege, *Philosophical and Mathematical Correspondence* (Chicago: University of Chicago Press, 1980), p. 132.

2. Thomas S. Kuhn, *The Structure of Scientific Revolutions*, 2d ed. (Chicago: University of Chicago Press, 1970), p. 135.

3. Zeno argued, for example, that in order to cross the room we would first have to cross half the room, but to do that we would have to cross half of that half. And so on ad infinitum. He concluded that any movement at all was impossible.

4. For an example of a physicist who does not accept the paradoxical interpretations of quantum mechanics, see P. R. Wallace, *Paradox Lost: Images of the Quantum* (New York: Springer, 1996).

5. E. E. Evans Pritchard, *Nuer Religion* (Oxford: Clarendon Press, 1956), pp. 128–31, cited in Alasdair MacIntyre, "Is Understanding Religion Compatible with Believing?" in Bryan R. Wilson, ed., *Rationality* (Oxford: Basil Blackwell, 1974), p. 65.

6. Thomas Nagel, *What Does It All Mean: A Very Short Introduction to Philosophy* (New York: Oxford University Press, 1987).

7. Bertrand Russell, *A History of Western Philosophy* (New York: Simon & Schuster, 1945).

8. Richard Rorty, "Does Academic Freedom Have Metaphysical Presuppositions?" *Academe* 80, no. 6 (November–December 1994): 57.

9. Richard Rorty, *Philosophy and the Mirror of Nature* (Princeton, N.J.: Princeton University Press, 1979), p. 275.

10. Hilary Putnam, *The Many Faces of Realism* (La Salle, Ill.: Open Court, 1987), p. 1.

11. Jacques Derrida, *Of Grammatology* (Baltimore: Johns Hopkins University Press, 1976), p. 158.

12. Richard Rorty, "The Priority of Democracy to Philosophy," in Merrill Peterson and Robert Vaughn, eds., *The Virginia Statute for Religious Freedom* (pp. 257–82), (Cambridge: Cambridge University Press, 1988), p. 271.

13. Nelson Goodman, *Of Mind and Other Matters* (Cambridge: Mass: Harvard University Press, 1984), p.36.

14. Brian Fay, *Contemporary Philosophy of Social Science* (Oxford: Blackwell, 1996), p. 72.

15. Ibid., p. 73.

16. The use-mention fallacy consists in confusing features of a word when it is mentioned with features of the thing referred to by the word when it is used. If I say, "'Berkeley' consists of eight letters," and, "Berkeley is a city in California," it is a fallacy to infer that there is a city in California that consists of eight letters. In the first sentence the word is mentioned, and in the second it is used to refer to a city.

17. Bruno Latour and Steve Woolgar, *Laboratory Life: The Construction of Scientific Facts*, 2d ed. (Princeton, N.J.: Princeton University Press, 1986), pp. 180–82.

18. Willard Van Orman Quine, "Two Dogmas of Empiricism," in *From a Logical Point of View* (Cambridge, Mass.: Harvard University Press, 1953), p. 44.

19. George Berkeley, *A Treatise Concerning the Principles of Human Knowledge* (Oxford: Oxford University Press, 1998).

20. Francis Crick, *The Astonishing Hypothesis* (New York: Scribner's/Maxwell Macmillan International, 1994), pp. 32–33.

21. David Hume, *A Treatise of Human Nature*, ed. L. A. Selby-Bigge (Oxford: Clarendon Press, 1888), pp. 210–11.

22. J. L. Austin, *Sense and Sensibilia* (Oxford: Oxford University Press, 1962).

Chapter 2

1. Thomas Nagel, "What It Is Like to Be a Bat," in *Mortal Questions* (Cambridge: Cambridge University Press, 1979), pp. 165–80.
2. Daniel Dennett, *Consciousness Explained* (Boston: Little, Brown, 1991).
3. Jean Piaget, *The Child's Conception of Physical Causality* (New York: Harcourt, Brace & Co., 1930).

Chapter 3

1. Michael Gazzaniga, *The Social Brain* (New York: Basic Books, 1985).
2. Daniel Schacter, *Searching for Memory* (New York: Basic Books, 1996).

Chapter 4

1. Jerry Fodor, *Psychosemantics: The Problem of Meaning in the Philosophy of Mind* (Cambridge, Mass.: MIT Press, 1987), p. 97.
2. Daniel Dennett, *Brainstorms* (Vermont: Bradford Books, 1978), pp. 122–24.
3. Fodor, *Psychosemantics*, pp. 97–127.
4. Perhaps the most extreme version of this tendency is to be found in Daniel Dennett's, *The Intentional Stance* (Cambridge, Mass.: MIT Press, 1987).
5. John L. Austin, "How to Talk: Some Simple Ways," in *Philosophical Papers*, edited by James O. Urmson and Geoffrey Warnock (Oxford: Clarendon Press, 1979).
6. G. E. M. Anscombe, *Intention* (Oxford: Blackwell, 1959).
7. The idea of causal self-referentiality is an old one and goes back at least to Kant. As far as I know, the term was first

used in Gilbert Harman, "Practical Reason," *Review of Metaphysics* 29, no. 3 (March 1976): 431–63.

Chapter 5

1. The idea was originally formulated by David Lewis in *Convention: A Philosophical Study* (Cambridge, Mass.: Harvard University Press, 1969), and Stephen Schiffer, *Meaning* (Oxford: Oxford University Press, 1972).

Chapter 6

1. J. L. Austin, *How to Do Things with Words* (Cambridge Mass.: Harvard University Press, 1962).
2. Paul Grice, "Meaning," *Philosophical Review* (July 1957): 377–88.

⇛ SUGGESTIONS FOR FURTHER READING

This reading list is for those who would like to pursue the issues raised in this book in more detail. It is for nonspecialists and is in no sense intended as a comprehensive philosophical bibliography of these issues. It is rather a continuation of and supplement to the references to works in the text. Many of the ideas in this book are developed more fully in earlier books by me, which I have included in the list.

First, you need a good philosophical dictionary or encyclopedia. There are now several good ones on the market. One I find useful is *The Cambridge Dictionary of Philosophy*, edited by Robert Audi (Cambridge: Cambridge University Press, 1995).

Second, it is a good idea to read some of the classic works that gave rise to many of the problems I address in the first three chapters of this book. The most important of these is René Descartes, *Meditations on First Philosophy*. Among the classics responding to Descartes' problems are George Berkeley's *Principles of Human Knowledge* and David Hume's *Treatise of Human Nature*, book 1. There are many editions of all of these books. I recommend them with some reluctance, because they are all in various ways massively confused, but they are historically very important.

Turning to the specific topics of this book:

Realism and Truth

There are surprisingly few recent defenses of the correspondence theory of truth or external realism. I tried to fill the gap in the last three chapters of John R. Searle, *The Construction of Social Reality* (New York: Free Press, 1995). William Alston, *A Realist Conception of Truth* (Ithaca, N.Y.: Cornell University Press, 1996), has a similar point of view.

Consciousness

There is a large number of recent books on consciousness. I reviewed several of these in

John R. Searle, *The Mystery of Consciousness* (New York: New York Review of Books, 1997). Two books by neuroscientists should be mentioned: Francis Crick, *The Astonishing Hypothesis: The Scientific Search for the Soul* (New York: Simon & Schuster, 1994), and Gerald Edelman, *Bright Air, Brilliant Fire: On the Matter of the Mind* (New York: Basic Books, 1992). Several others are Owen Flanagan, *Consciousness Reconsidered* (Cambridge, Mass: MIT Press, 1992). Colin McGinn, *The Problem of Consciousness* (Oxford: Basil Blackwell, 1991), and Bernard Baars, *A Cognitive Theory of Consciousness* (Cambridge: Cambridge University Press, 1988). A useful collection of readings is edited by Ned Block, Owen Flanagan, and Guven Guzeldere, *The Nature of Consciousness: Philosophical Debates* (Cambridge, Mass.: MIT Press, 1997). Other books about mental phenomena generally are John R. Searle, *The Rediscovery of the Mind* (Cambridge, Mass.: MIT Press, 1992), John R. Searle, *Minds, Brains and Science* (Cambridge, Mass.: Harvard University Press, 1984), Galen Strawson, *Mental Reality* (Cambridge, Mass.: MIT Press, 1994), and Thomas Nagel, *The View from Nowhere* (New York: Oxford University Press, 1986).

Intentionality

For a comprehensive theory of intentionality, see:

John R. Searle, *Intentionality: An Essay in the Philosophy of Mind* (Cambridge: Cambridge University Press, 1983). On the problem of the Background, see especially Ludwig Wittgenstein, *On Certainty* (New York: Harper & Row, 1969). Also see his classic *Philosophical Investigations* (Oxford: Basil Blackwell, 1953).

Meaning and Speech Acts

The founding text on the theory of speech acts is:

John L. Austin, *How to Do Things with Words* (Cambridge, Mass.: Harvard University Press, 1962). Some other standard works are John R. Searle, *Speech Acts: An Essay in the Philosophy of Language* (Cambridge: Cambridge University Press, 1969), John R. Searle, *Expression and Meaning: Essays in the Theory of Speech Acts* (Cambridge: Cambridge University Press, 1979), and Paul Grice, *Studies in the Way of Words* (Cambridge, Mass.: Harvard University Press, 1989).

Social Reality

Two of the classic authors who struggled with the issues related to those discussed in this book are:

Max Weber, *Economy and Society*, in first part of volume 1 (Berkeley: University of California Press, 1978), and

George Herbert Mead, *Mind, Self, and Society* (Chicago: University of Chicago Press, 1970). My views are developed in John R. Searle, *The Construction of Social Reality* (New York: Free Press, 1995).

�361SUBJECT INDEX

⟹NAME INDEX